CONTENT MACHINE

CONTENT MACHINE

USE CONTENT MARKETING TO BUILD A 7-FIGURE BUSINESS WITH ZERO ADVERTISING

DAN NORRIS

FOREWORD BY NEIL PATEL

ISBN-10: 1515213439
ISBN-13: 978-1515213437

Join Other Entrepreneurs and Build Your Content Machine

There's a lot covered in this book, and many of these topics are better discussed with a community of likeminded entrepreneurs.

If you are serious about implementing what you learn in this book, I'd love to have you in my private community. It's where I hang out with entrepreneurs and content marketers who get shit done.

Every day we dissect different topics around entrepreneurship, with a focus on online and content marketing.

Visit http://contentmachine.com/community to check it out, I'll see you there.

CONTENTS

FOREWORD
BY NEIL PATEL

To say I have committed to content marketing as a key strategy in business would be a huge understatement.

As a content creator I'm a natural and passionate educator. I've been actively creating content for my businesses for over eight years. Even though it was a slow start, I have now used it to build four multi-million dollar businesses.

There's no doubt content marketing is powerful, but it's not easy. The messages, specific instruction, and associated resources in this book will help you do it right.

I started content marketing because I couldn't afford to pay for advertising. Writing a blog post was free, so I wrote a post called "Got Crunched" about being featured on Techcrunch. I figured I'd get some traffic from the popular news site Digg.com, and I'd get some attention for my business.

Good news—I got the traffic. Bad news—it didn't stick. So I kept at it, and worked tirelessly on creating content that people cared about.

My first successful post was about 75 designer resources. It was a detailed list of specific things that designers could use. This post was much more successful than others I'd written, and I knew I was onto something.

My plan evolved into writing detailed, highly actionable, long, and practical content.

I've written countless 5,000+ word posts on virtually every online marketing topic you can think of on my sites: **Kissmetrics** (http://blog.kissmetrics.com) and **Crazy Egg** (http://blog.crazyegg.com). I've even done some 20,000- and 30,000-word guides on **Quick Sprout** (http://quicksprout.com). Any time I can think of a project that can be more practical, more useful, more detailed, and more actionable, I will do it.

As a result, I've built blogs with millions of visitors and turned that attention into multi-million dollar business results for my companies.

My approach is to go above and beyond others to get noticed, and that is certainly what has happened. As Dan will address in *Content Machine*, it's not enough to create great content. You have to create content so much better than your competition that you really stand out.

There is no point at all in generating mediocre content. Don't just write about your business or your product. Your content has to be educational and solve problems.

Talk to potential customers and figure out what they want. Throw away everything you learned in school. Writing content is a two-way conversation, not a speech. Be personal and make people feel like you are there with them.

Selflessly help your customers. Give the Zappos experience through education.

This is how you get noticed, how you truly help people, and it's how you create content that people care about.

Doing it just for keyword rankings or to hit quotas is a frivolous exercise.

Content Machine will show you exactly how to do all this, and much more.

All the best in your content marketing journey.

Neil Patel
Entrepreneur and Passionate Content Creator

INTRODUCTION

"If you suck at sales, can you be an entrepreneur?"

From 2002 to 2006, when I was working a job, I assumed the answer was no.

The entrepreneurs I looked up to, like Richard Branson and Steve Jobs, seemed to be epic salespeople. I figured entrepreneurship wasn't for me. Besides, my job was good, my income was going up every year, and things were okay.

But in 2006 I did start a business. My income took a big hit, and I continued to ask myself this question for the next eight years. I asked it every day in the seven years of my first business, a failed web agency. I asked it every day in the year of my second business, a failed software startup.

I asked it for the last time on June 27, 2013.

In the year prior, I'd spent $60,000 to buy 12 months of runway for my software startup. I had two weeks left, was losing $1,500/month, and found myself in the process of starting to look for jobs.

It was my lowest point as an entrepreneur. I'd decided that maybe I wasn't an entrepreneur after all. My kids were at the age where they were starting to ask what I did for a living. What would I tell them?

It's now June 2015. In the last few months I've spoken as a business expert in five cities around the world, I have a best-selling book on Amazon, and I run four businesses; including one of the fastest growing WordPress support companies in the world, WP Curve. We have built a team of over 45 developers in seven countries, worked with over 4,000 clients, and turn over a million or more in Australian dollars per year.

My income chart looks like one hell of a rollercoaster ride:

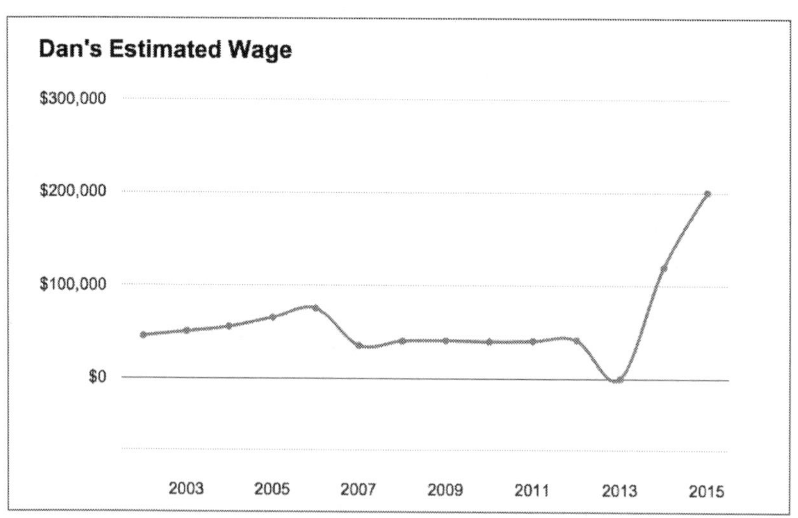

In the end, I figured out I could be an entrepreneur. And I still suck at sales.

You Are Lucky!

If you had been born just one generation ago and I had told you there was a way to build a million-dollar business without spending a cent on advertising, while at the same time helping thousands of people, you would have told me I was crazy.

Yet here we are. The most powerful and valuable form of marketing is at your fingertips, freely available and almost free to use.

“Sure,” you say, “it’s easier than ever to create content, but there’s also way more competition.”

Really? Take a look at your top three or four competitors and see what sort of quality they are putting out. I’d be willing to bet it’s not great.

If that’s the case, you have a huge opportunity waiting for you. This book will help you take it.

I’m on a plane writing this—my second book—only two weeks after the launch of my first, *The 7 Day Startup*. I gave away 13,000 free copies of that book on Amazon Kindle in the first week. It took me six months to put together, including 200+ emails to both my editor and my formatter.

Giving it away was an easy decision, because it's what I do with all of my projects: create lots of useful content, give it away for free, and use that attention to build a business.

I've taken this approach from day one of my WordPress website support service, WP Curve. In the two years since we launched, we've spent a total of $181.23 on advertising, and haven't done anything that would represent traditional "sales" work.

Instead of paid advertising, I focused on creating content and giving it away for free. *The 7 Day Startup* was only a tiny exercise compared to all of the content I've put together over the years. In fact, at 26,000 words, it represents just 4% of the total amount. Since 2008 I've written around 600,000 words, which adds up to a book longer than *War and Peace*. I haven't charged a cent for any of it.

We still don't spend money on advertising for WP Curve. We have a full time content manager, paid guest writers, and continue to focus on content marketing as our only marketing strategy.

Content Machine will show you how to do the same thing. I just don't want it to take you two years and half a million words to get there.

Quality Over Quantity

I was flying blind when I first started content marketing. I followed the general "write every day" advice and focused too much on the amount of content I was creating. The problem was, 90% of it went pretty much unnoticed.

In this book I'm going to show you a simple, three-piece framework for ensuring this doesn't happen to you. For now, let's go through some of my early numbers:

- Since 2008, I've created around 700 pieces of content.
- At least 400 of those were in the last two years.
- I've sent an email to my list almost every week.
- I wrote about 350 on-site articles before I had an article with more than 10 tweets (that should be ringing alarm bells).
- Almost every article I wrote prior to two years ago still has less than ten tweets, with only a handful with just over.
- I didn't really start believing we could build a business using content marketing until last year!

I invested too much time in every type of content you can imagine:

- I did intense content creation sessions, including one in August 2012 where I wrote 13 articles in one day.
- In one week of December 2012, I launched a new podcast, created ten podcast episodes, wrote six blog posts, and appeared on three other sites.

- I spent weeks working on single pieces of content that got less than 100 total views.

I ran webinars; created free plugins; designed infographics; commissioned funny illustrations; recorded podcasts; produced videos; wrote long posts (5,000+ words); crafted interactive/graphic content; created detailed step-by-step marketing guides; built email courses and sequences (some as long as 52 emails); developed video training; wrote guest posts; composed interactive guest posts; combined writing, illustration, and audio; recorded hundreds of guest interviews; presented at conferences; wrote media releases, ebooks, and books; targeted articles at press outlets; conducted significant influencer outreach; answered questions in forums; did AMAs; and much, much more.

You name it, I've tried it.

I loved creating the content, but there was a problem. I measured myself based on how much content I created, not how much traction that content got. The quantity, not the quality.

Like Neil Patel, I eventually worked out that one spectacularly successful piece of content was infinitely more valuable than 100 pieces of content that go unnoticed.

By using the tools in this book, you will hopefully get the fun without the struggle.

Throughout the years I've become passionate about content marketing. I've helped other people build their businesses with content, and I've reached out to people who are getting great results with their own content.

Most people don't see great returns—in fact, according to the 2015 Content Marketing Institute (CMI) research on business to business marketers, only 38% regard their content marketing as effective.[1] The respondees are mostly CMI members, so you can imagine what the average business owner thinks.

I've made it my mission to ensure you are not one of the people who regards content marketing as ineffective.

This book will help you achieve a few things:

First, you will fully understand what content marketing is and how a working content marketing strategy is put together. You may decide it's not for you, or you may jump in headfirst, screeching with excitement. Either way, you need to understand it before you decide.

Second, you will learn a simple three-step framework for content marketing success. It will help you focus on the right things, as opposed to simply "writing every day."

On top of that, I'll make your life easier by providing a number of downloadable frameworks and assets that you can plug into your business immediately to ensure your content marketing strategy is effective.

Start Taking Action on Content Marketing Now

I'm big on taking action. I hope you take action with this book, be it by creating a blog, re-working some old content, or releasing a podcast. If you implement one idea or like a quote in this book, I'd appreciate if you could share it with the #contentmachine hashtag on Twitter or Instagram. You can tag me if you like (@thedannorris). I love re-sharing the mentions, and it's great for me to see what parts of the book are having an impact. I've also put together a bunch of resources for this book to support every chapter. Visit http://contentmachine.com/resources for free access to frameworks, resources, quotes, and every link mentioned in the book. I want this to be the most actionable book on content marketing in the world. I want to show you specific examples of entrepreneurs who have made content marketing work, and then give you the tools to do the same for yourself. In short, regardless of your experience with online content right now, my goal is for you to finish this book and be in a position to build a high-growth business without spending a cent on advertising.

Let's get started.

Notes

1. Joe Pulizzi, "New B2B Content Marketing Research: Focus on Documenting Your Strategy," *Content Marketing Institute*, Z Squared Media LLC, last modified October 1, 2014, http://contentmarketinginstitute.com/2014/10/2015-b2b-content-marketing-research/.

CHAPTER 1

HOW TO BUILD A BUSINESS WITH CONTENT MARKETING

Let's start with a super simple definition for content marketing:

Content marketing is releasing something interesting that grabs attention for a business and builds trust.

That's it! Easy, right?

For some companies, like Red Bull, it means hundreds of staff in professional studios creating multi-million dollar feature films and releasing them for free. For others it means writing blog posts, putting recipes and nice images on Instagram, or recording a podcast.

The most important pieces of the content marketing definition are attention and trust.

You want to put out content that helps people, gets them to pay attention to you and your business, and, over time, garners their trust. These people become part of your community, they help promote your content, refer people to your business, and may even become partners or customers.

This book is a form of content marketing. If you are reading it, I have your attention. By the end, you will feel like you know me, and you will trust me more than you did before. You will know of my businesses and you will be part of my worldwide community of passionate content marketers.

The idea has been around for hundreds of years. One of the earliest recognized forms of content marketing was a magazine started in 1895 by John Deere called *The Furrow*. It provided interesting information about farming and built a worldwide following for the brand which continues to this day.

With the emergence of the web and social media, content marketing has exploded. The core idea is the same, but the methods for doing it—and, more importantly, doing it well—have changed dramatically.

Are You a Blogger or a Content Marketer?

So you're fired up about content marketing and ready to start or improve on your own content strategy.

But first, I'm going to fill you in on some bad news. I get hundreds of comments and emails from people who are frustrated because, for the vast majority, content marketing does not seem to work.

Out of all the failure I see, I can narrow almost all of it down with one simple question:

> If I were to ask you what the most important task as a content marketer is, what would you say?

How about you? Did you say "creating content" or "blogging"?

If you did, then you made the mistake that most failed content marketers make. You see yourself as a creator of content or a blogger but you don't see yourself as a marketer.

You have assumed that your job is to create content, when really your job is to market a business.

Luckily this book isn't a book on how to write blog posts. It's a book about how to build a business using content marketing. Let's look at how that works. There are 3 components.

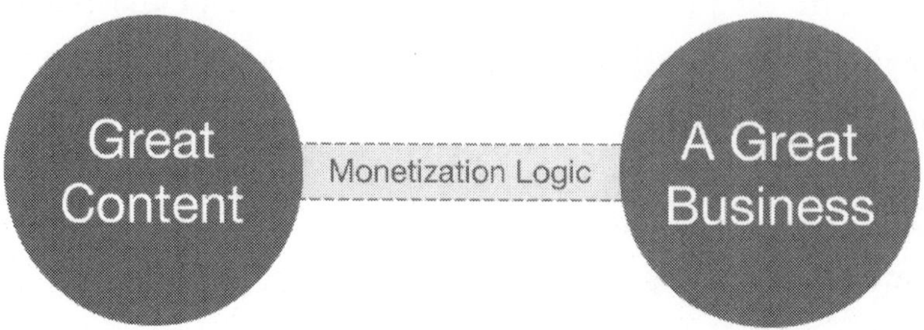

Of course you need great content that grabs the attention of your audience and builds their trust. The ability to identify what great content is and do it at scale on an ongoing basis is what the majority of this book focuses on.

Creating great content is not enough, because without a great business, you are sending attention to something that is broken (or non-existent).

Finally there needs to be a logical link between the two. I call this Monetization Logic. I will talk more about that towards the end of this chapter. For now let's look at how to build a great business.

10 Characteristics Of A High-Growth Business

After nine years of entrepreneurship, I've had a lot of ups and downs. I've had businesses that completely failed, one that stagnated for seven years, and others that grew to multiple six-figures in under a year. I've learned that some businesses are fundamentally designed to grow and some are not. I've paid particular attention to the startup world where growth is worshipped while staying away from accepted small business advice.

Through my own experience and observations of other successful companies, especially those I covered in my first book, *The 7 Day Startup*, I've narrowed these traits down to 10 Characteristics of High-Growth Companies. If these are not present in your business, you will struggle to make any form of marketing work.

When someone isn't able to grow their business from high-quality, differentiated, scalable content marketing, something is fundamentally flawed in the way the business is designed. They lack one or all of these characteristics.

I see these traits in businesses that are designed to scale without their founders. If you are going to focus on building a content machine, you need something that will grow without your constant attention.

Some of these things might challenge you. Not everyone wants to build a high-growth startup. However, rather than dismissing them right away, I encourage you to take some time to consider the possible implications for your business. If there are things you can apply to create a more sound business, it makes sense to implement them now so you get a better return from your content marketing.

1. They Are Fundamentally Profitable

What happens when the business expands, and the founder *isn't* capable of doing all the work anymore?

If the profit margin in your business is set so you are unable to replace yourself and still make a profit, then you are in trouble. Despite what you may hear, it's not an easy problem to solve. You think you can just raise prices, but that may send your customers to more affordable competitors. Your business might be fundamentally unprofitable.

Here's a very simple calculation I recommend every business owner should perform: Figure out everything that goes into serving a customer. How many hours will you need from X, Y, and Z staff members to complete the tasks, and how much do those staff members cost. Imagine your business is at a reasonable size, and that you have all of the tools and technologies necessary to manage a decent number of clients. Distribute the costs across those clients to come up with a rough idea of how much it's going to cost to deliver your service. Take that number and, at the very least, double it. That is your price.

Charge that much now, and see if your business grows. If it doesn't, you might have a problem—and no amount of content is going to fix a fundamentally unprofitable business.

Pricing is a complicated topic in itself, but many businesses haven't done this basic calculation, and they end up running fundamentally unprofitable businesses. Then they wonder why their content marketing isn't building them a profitable business.

2. They Operate In A Large Market

Common business advice tells you to find a small niche and go after it. I don't like this advice, and I don't see successful high-growth companies doing it.

The main difference between my first business and my third was the size of the market we were in. My first, the failed web agency, targeted mainly local businesses in my geographical area. My third, WP Curve, is available to anyone in the world who uses WordPress (70 million websites).

Being in a large market has resulted in constant, high, and at times almost unmanageable growth. It also means we can be broad with our content and build a lot of support from a large community.

Your content marketing is often available to the whole world. If you can figure out a way for your business to be just as available, then your content will have much more power.

3. They Naturally Build Assets Over Time

All high-growth companies have some sort of assets that set them apart from their competition. It could be the IP for software; it could be their people; it could be their brand. This is something that small businesses don't often think about, but investors in large companies obsess over.

The question they ask is, "What is stopping someone else from coming along and taking what you have?" This is very difficult for a small business to build on when they are starting out, but it's something worth thinking about for the future. Is your business structured in a way that makes it extremely easy for competitors to come along and do the same thing? Can customers just leave and go somewhere else without any difficulty?

If that's the case, what can you do about it? Can you invest in your brand, your people, or something else? Can you get legal protections like trademarks? Can you build technical expertise or something physical and tangible?

4. They Have a Simple, Relatable Differentiator

I noticed that high-growth companies tend to go after existing problems, and they solve them with a unique twist. This means they don't have to convince people of the fundamental problem—people are paying for a solution already. They just have to stand out with one major differentiating factor, and ideally it will be one people will talk about because they care about it.

Here are some examples:

- WP Curve: Like a developer **except** unlimited fixes 24/7.
- Uber: Like taxis **except** cleaner, safer, cheaper, nice smelling, and they actually arrive.
- Airbnb: Like hotels **except** you get more for less.
- Trello: Like post-it notes, **except** on your computer.
- Evernote: Like your brain, **except** you can't forget.

If the part after the "except" is something customers care about enough to talk about, then you are off to a good start. If your business has no differentiating aspect, or has one that customers don't care about and won't talk about, then you are in trouble.

5. They Focus On Growing Consistent Revenue At a High Lifetime Value

Not all revenue is equal. Predictability in business is highly underrated. Businesses that are successful in the long term generally have a predictable revenue model. Those categorized by huge peaks and troughs, one-off launches, and up-and-down months are far more difficult.

If you operate a business with monthly consistent revenue (ideally recurring), then everything is much easier. You can invest in tools, technology, and people that you need to grow, because you are confident you will be able to afford it next month. You can say "no" to certain customers or projects, because you already have a good solid base of revenue. You can accurately estimate your profit margin and your cashflow.

If your business is cyclical and inconsistent in revenue, think about how you can *make* it more consistent. Making less money on a recurring monthly basis might be a better long-term option, as long as you still have an acceptable profit margin.

It's also important that over time, you make a reasonable amount of money from each customer (called Lifetime Value). Building a business by selling a one off $20 product is going to be a lot tougher than a business that sells an $80 monthly subscription. If you don't have a reasonable lifetime value, you won't get adequate reward for your hard work getting the attention and building the trust.

6. They Invest In A Memorable Brand

Design and general execution is one of the most underrated marketing strategies in business. I've noticed that most successful new companies have very short, memorable, and well-executed brands. They fall easily into conversation, and they spread via word of mouth like wildfire.

Think about: "We caught an Uber," "Put it in Slack," etc.

Make sure you have thought about building a real brand in your business. Not just a website with a bunch of keywords in it, but a strong brand—ideally short and memorable—that is well executed with world-class design that stands for specific values. People want to fall in love with brands, so don't skimp out on this aspect in your business. No one will ever *tell* you they decided to use a competitor because they didn't trust your overall design, but it happens constantly.

Remember that you aren't a designer. Once you are up and running, this is something you need to take seriously and get some real help on—and not from your friends on Facebook.

Find a designer who can execute something of top quality for you, so you can truly compete or even stand out from the competition.

The best part is that content is a huge brand builder. If you can focus on your design and keep your content at the same level, pushing a similar message, design, and content can work together explosively.

7. They Are Started By A Team, Not An Individual

A lot of solo entrepreneurs struggle with the same issue: the founder is responsible for too many different jobs. That works only as long as the founder is capable of doing those jobs.

It's extremely rare for a decent company to be built by an individual and not a founding team. Just look at the startup world for guidance.

- Almost every startup I can think of had a founding team.
- Paul Graham, the founder of Y Combinator and one of the world's leading startup experts, cites "single founder" as the top item in his list of why startups fail.
- Incubators that are designed to find the highest potential customers, invest in them, and grow them rarely accept a company without a founding team.
- Investors will rarely invest in a startup with one founder.
- An individual with all of the necessary skills to run a great business is like a unicorn. Maybe they exist? Maybe they don't? I've never met one.
- Like every entrepreneur, I tend to think I can do everything and am "a jack of all trades". But I had zero success until I started businesses with other people.

- Running a business is an emotional rollercoaster of epic proportions. You can't ride it alone—get someone else on board.

Think long and hard about this one. Can you realistically be an epic entrepreneur as well as a world class content marketer?

When I started WP Curve, I agreed to give half of the company away so I could start it with someone else. In two years, the company became five times the size that my last business was after *seven* years. I would rather own 50% of a million-dollar company than 100% of a $150k company.

8. They Know How To Say "No," And They Do It Often

Great businesses choose what they are going to do, and they do it extremely well. It takes a long time, generally a lot of people, and a lot of money to truly achieve "world class" status. If your business has multiple focuses rather than one main task, it might be a sign that you are in trouble. You might not have enough confidence in your ability to meet a world-class standard and attract enough customers.

Bolting more sub-par solutions onto your main service will not solve that problem—it will only complicate your business and increase the likelihood of running into a fundamentally unprofitable model.

Learn how to say “no”. Instead, reach “world class” status at one thing. Be confident that you can use your content marketing skills to get so much attention for this one thing that there will be plenty of demand.

9. They Understand The Power Of Monthly Growth

I mentioned consistent revenue above, but let me illustrate the power of monthly growth with an example. Say your business is currently doing $6,000 per month, and it’s growing at 15% every month.

After two years, you will have a two-million-dollar annual business.

After three years, you will have a ten-million-dollar annual business.

Of course, nothing is ever as simple as growing from two to ten million in one year. However, it illustrates the power of monthly growth. Great businesses understand this and they obsess over it.

Don’t think so much about how much money you will make in a year. Think about how much you will grow every single month, and before you know it your business will be significantly bigger.

This is also a great way to think about the metrics for your content. I noticed our blog traffic grew by about 5% per month in the early days. At first it didn't seem like much, but with consistent monthly growth, before we knew it, we had tens of thousands of monthly visitors.

10. They Think "Long Term"

Great businesses avoid get-rich-quick schemes and over-optimization. They focus on solid, long-term strategies.

Getting in the press, building a public profile, putting out useful content, fostering important relationships, and developing a great company culture are all examples of solid long-term strategies. These aren't going to result in quick wins, but they *are* what creates great companies.

Think about these things from the day you start your business and act as if you are building a brand that you can pass onto your children. This will drive you to excellence and steer you away from the latest marketing fads that probably won't work for you anyway.

Think about all of these characteristics and how you can build them into your own business. If your content isn't getting the results you want, think about whether there is something fundamental here that needs to be addressed.

Don't forget to review these characteristics step by step and make sure the business you build is worth sending leads to.

Monetization Logic

Sometimes content marketing fails because the business is fundamentally broken. Other times it fails because the content is not good enough. But content marketing can also fail if both the business and the content are sound. This happens when the business strategy includes poor monetization logic. That is, there is no logical link between the content and the business.

Monetization logic is a simple "Yeah that makes sense" test that is often missing from people's content marketing efforts. The easiest way to determine whether it exists is to ask the question, "Does it make sense that someone would consume this content and then go on to become a customer?"

Let's look at some examples.

Moz (https://moz.com/blog) has a great blog with useful content about how to rank well in Google. Their business is selling software to help people rank well in Google. So it makes sense that someone interested in content about ranking well in Google would also be interested in buying software that helps them rank well in Google. This is an example of strong monetization logic and they've built a $30m business off the back of their content.

Intercom (https://blog.intercom.io/) has a great blog with useful content about how to build software companies.

Their business is a messaging app for software companies. So it makes sense that someone interested in building a software company would also be interested in using their messaging software. Again, this is great monetization logic.

If Moz created content about building a software company, it wouldn't work nearly as well because it doesn't make sense. If Intercom created content about ranking well in Google, that wouldn't translate into a good stream of leads.

Another example where people get monetization logic wrong is geographically. Say you run a local agency that builds websites for bricks and mortar businesses. You have an internationally popular design blog that breaks down the amazing design work you do. It might get huge worldwide traction, but it fails the monetization logic test. Most of the people who see the content aren't local and therefore can't become a customer. It's also failing at a topic level because it will appeal to designers, and designers won't become customers of another design firm.

It doesn't mean you have to specifically create content only for your customers, but it does mean it has to generally make sense.

There needs to be a logical link between your content, your audience, and whatever it is you are selling. A decent percentage of your audience should be potential customers or potentially refer other customers to your service. If they aren't, then the monetization logic is off.

Think about this as you grow your content marketing strategy. Does it make sense that consumers of your content would help your business (by becoming customers or referring customers), or does something need to be tweaked to make sure this logic is in place?

The Content Marketing Leap of Faith

Okay, so where are we at?

You know the basics of content marketing and why it often fails. You understand you need great content, a great business, and a logical link between them.

You are good to go, right?

Not quite. There's one more reality check.

The content marketing leap of faith.

There's another important reason why people fail at content marketing. It's a reason that is visible on the Google Analytics charts of most successful blogs. They look something like this.

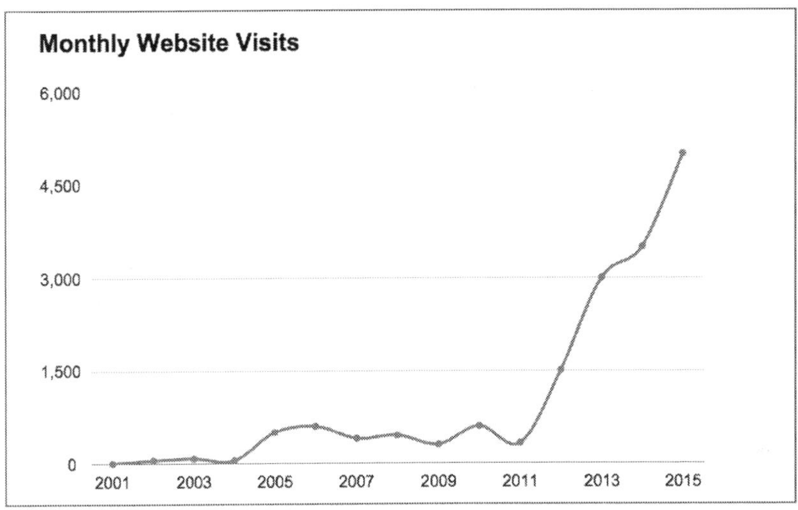

Hopefully you spotted it: they give up too soon. It takes a long time to build momentum, and most people don't have the patience to back something that isn't delivering immediate results.

Content marketing, by its nature, is a long-term exercise. Most top blogs create content for months or years before they hit traction. This is the norm, and there are a few reasons for it.

1. Content marketing is about building trust, and you can't build trust overnight. Trust is crucial online. People won't rush to read and share new sites. You have to earn trust over time, and you do that by consistently building your content brand. Unless you are a well-known entrepreneur, you are going to have to do the work.

2. It takes a while for some channels to kick in. For example, Google favors older sites with more links and more content. If we create an article right now on WordPress speed, it will rank well. But if we did that in our first week of business, it wouldn't rank at all. As it turns out, we do have an article on WordPress speed that was written some time ago. That particular article got 5,000 visits just from Google last month. It's hard to place a value on that amount of free traffic just for one article. We get tens of thousands of visitors every month to posts that were written years ago.
3. It takes a long time to endear a valuable community member. Much like physical communities, you can't just waltz in and expect to be at the top right away. It takes time for *you* to learn what the community members like and for *them* to learn that you are a valuable contributor.
4. It takes time to find your place. I've mentioned how critical it is to work out your core vision and work out what your audience loves. This is hard to do quickly, and you should expect some trial and error on that journey.
5. Good content breeds more good content. It could be the value gained by linking between blog posts, doing guest content on topics that went well on your site, or doing another post similar to one that did well on your site. Whatever it is, there is an "economies of

> scale" effect with content marketing. As you create content and you craft some winners, it becomes a lot easier to get more.

I experienced this myself in the years between 2008 and 2013. I really struggled to find my place, had patchy results, and created a lot of content that didn't result in much benefit. In 2013 I hit my stride. I released a bunch of posts that garnered over 200 tweets each and thousands of visits; I started getting mentioned on my favorite podcasts; I appeared on other posts as a guest author; and I was voted as Australia's top small business blogger by the readers of *Smarter Business Ideas Magazine*.

Before 2013, the highest number of monthly visits I had ever gotten to the site was 5,000. In 2013 I was getting 10,000 per month, and in 2014 I was getting 60,000 per month.

At some point along the way, I had to take a leap of faith. I had to accept that it was going to take me a long time to figure out how to get big results from the content, but I *would* figure it out. I trusted myself to work out what content I loved creating and how to best position it on my site. I worked through the void of limited results to our current position of ultimate competitive advantage, where we can acquire customers without spending a cent.

With the lessons in this book, you can get there quicker than I did. But it won't happen overnight.

Take the leap of faith.

CHAPTER 2

CONTENT MARKETING BASICS

The rest of this book is dedicated to helping you create high-quality content that grabs attention, builds trust, differentiates you from your competitors, and can be scaled.

Let's start with a content marketing strategy.

There are some things that are non-negotiable when it comes to creating great content, which is why I have found that drafting a content strategy, before you dig into plans and execution, is a good move. Remember, you don't want to spit out just any content at a rapid speed. You want to do it with direction.

The 10-Minute Content Strategy

Like a lot of entrepreneurs, I find it more natural to "wing it" than have things documented all the time. Still, when it comes to a content marketing strategy, it makes sense to write it down. When you are on your own, you might get by with a "make it up as you go" approach. If you want to build a real long-term machine, you need to remove yourself from the process at some point. You need to define a strategy and then build processes around that strategy.

I've included a free ten-minute content marketing strategy template at http://contentmachine.com/resources for you to work through. Here are the components:

- Vision – What is your blog about when it reaches its full potential?
- Values – What are the key values that will inform your content choices? You can refine these over time. They will end up being a blend of your personal philosophy and what has worked well with your audience.
- Inspirations – Where do you look for inspiration (design, content, voice, etc.)? These can be direct competitors or people in a totally separate industry.
- Strategy Comment – Do you have a high-level description of the overall strategy behind the blog? Do your best to come up with something now, but it will be easier to refine this after you have finished this book, particularly the "Building The Machine" chapter.
- Target Communities – What groups of people are you creating content for, and where do they hang out?

- Differentiators – How will this blog be different from what is already available? You might have a handle on this now, or you may refine it over time as you learn what's working.
- Unfair Advantage – What about you, your business, your style, your team, etc. gives you an advantage? Again, you might know this now, or you might notice it over time as people start engaging with your content.
- Key Relationships – Who are the big influencers capable of boosting your content if you get them on board? These will be the ones who have a decently sized audience within the types of communities you are going after. I find normally it's not that hard to figure out who these people are. If you are struggling, check out **Followerwonk** (https://followerwonk.com/) or **Little Bird** (http://www.getlittlebird.com/).
- Metrics – How will you know when your content is successful? If in doubt, use my three key metrics of total shares, comments, and email replies (more on these later).
- Lead Magnets and CTAs (Calls to Action) – What items can you use to encourage people to opt in, and what will your CTA be? This may change after you've been through the "Building The Machine" chapter, but for now, think about a downloadable you can give away to entice people to sign up for your

emails, or simply create a nice banner ad that aims to get people on your main landing page.

The template provided at http://contentmachine.com/resources includes instructions and enables you to create your own strategy in ten minutes. Most of the areas are fairly self-explanatory, but let's delve into two that require some further reinforcement.

Your Content Vision

It's going to be very hard to make a content marketing strategy work if you aren't clear on the end game. A good way to think about your vision is answering the question, "What will I/we stand for?"

When I started WP Curve, I knew the world didn't need more marketing blogs. It certainly didn't need more "How To" WordPress blogs. There wasn't a lot of unique value to offer there.

However, I knew my entrepreneurial friends and I needed more "real" entrepreneurial content. By creating a lot of content in this space, I gradually found a voice that really appealed to other entrepreneurs. Themes began to emerge.

My income reports got a lot of attention, because I'd delve into incredible detail about what decisions I was making at what stage of the business. Entrepreneurs could relate to it and were fascinated with what I was doing. Often they didn't agree, and they left passionate replies to that effect. But they were interested. They were engaged. Radical transparency became a theme.

My stories about my previous failed businesses have resonated well. Entrepreneurs have ups and downs—they don't want to see only success stories; they want to know what others have learned along the way. Some of my deepest content has been about when I was struggling through difficult times, and that has had a great impact on my audience. Deep emotional connection also became a theme.

Our blog has turned into a place where bootstrapped startups can get real advice about how to start, grow, and market a business. We don't post the typical fluff you find on other similarly-themed sites. We post detailed lessons learned from the trenches of our own business and others. We began to notice that the highly tactical, actionable, detailed, step-by-step content resonated well. Actionable content then became another main theme.

These themes turned into a vision of a blog where entrepreneurs could come for real, transparent business advice; real-life entrepreneurial stories; and highly actionable, applicable resources.

We release intimate details about our own business, including our income, our traffic stats, our team size, our revenue/costs, etc. People love this sort of content, because it makes everything *real* for them.

We interview other entrepreneurs and learn how they started, got through the rough times, and ultimately grew their businesses.

Giving away detailed processes or tools that have helped us grow is another important factor. For example, they get to see our policies on hiring developers or managing guest authors. This is useful for other entrepreneurs, and it's not the typical content you get on startup blogs. If you are interested in checking some of these out, I've added the top posts on http://contentmachine.com/resources.

I believe a lot of information you get from business books and traditional "expert" business channels is generic and boring. I wanted to resolve that with a blog that provides something interesting, up-to-date, and real.

This philosophy emerged as the vision behind the WP Curve blog.

What is the vision for your content? What will separate it from others in your industry? What do you believe will influence your content strategy?

In short, what do you believe people want that they aren't currently getting?

You may not have a clear idea about this at first, but keep coming back to the vision as you go through this book and, over time as you create more content, something will emerge that will give you a unique edge and take your content to the next level.

Here are a few examples from other businesses to give you some more ideas:

Kathryn Minshew started **The Muse** (http://themuse.com) because she believed that people hunting for jobs wanted to seek out companies, not the other way around. They were looking for a place where they could gain intimate details about working at a company, but no such place existed. So Kathryn created one. The Muse films in-depth and high-production value videos for companies to demonstrate what it's like to work there. Job seekers can then find those videos, and their ideal employer, in the process. It flipped the traditional hiring model on its head.

Buffer (https://buffer.com/) believes in radical transparency in business. Entrepreneurs want real, in-depth detail about what is happening inside a business to make better decisions about their own. There were no good places for them to get this information. So Joel and Leo created it.

Their website has a live dashboard that displays all of their key company financial metrics to the public. Everything from revenue, to churn, to growth. They provide in-depth details about how much they pay staff and why, how much they spend on staff retreats, and how they manage their people.

They are a multi-million dollar funded company with thousands of customers. Since day one, they have executed this vision to have one of the most successful startup blogs in the world.

Tim Ferriss (http://fourhourworkweek.com/) believes there are more efficient ways to break down success and learn what works. He didn't believe there was a good place for people to go to find out these hacks. So he created one.

On his blog, he interviews people and has guests share lengthy (5,000+ words) posts about their processes in goal achievement. He treats himself like a human guinea pig and has created best-selling books and a TV show on the topic. All of the content he creates is loosely based around this theme, and he's defined a clear space that he leads in that area.

Dave Asprey (https://www.bulletproofexec.com/) believes that traditional diet and exercise advice is harmful for mental performance. He believes you can change your life and "upgrade" yourself with simple diet and exercise “hacks”. He believes people want to discover this info from alternative sources and didn’t believe there was a good place for people to do so. So he created one.

His website has a blog with millions of readers, a top-ranking podcast, best-selling books, and downloadable resources on a range of topics around his central theme. Plus, he’s built a seven-figure business mainly selling supplements, like Bulletproof Coffee, off the back of his content.

Success stories aren’t limited to the big name entrepreneurs, either. In some cases, content can deliver amazing results on a very small scale. This has been the case for my latest business, **Black Hops Brewing** (http://blackhops.com.au), a craft beer producer on Gold Coast, Australia. In Differentiation, I’ll go into detail about how we’ve attracted investors, local newspapers, conference invitations, customers, and partners all from only eleven blog posts on the site. We’ve done it, because we believe it should be easy for keen brewers to find information on everything they need to get into the craft beer scene in Australia, and currently they can’t.

In these examples, people aren’t simply writing blog posts. They have defined a community to help, and they are executing on a broad vision. They believe something about what people want and aren’t currently getting. And they are using their unique advantage to fill that gap.

That is the essence of an effective content marketing vision.

What is your vision? What place do you fill in your market? What do you want people to think of when they think of your brand? What do you believe people want that they aren't currently getting?

This might be something you are clear on from the start, or perhaps you'll build this over time as you learn what works. Maybe you see an unmet need or maybe you are passionate about a subject that you like to talk about. Keep coming back to this and work on a unique vision for your content. It will impact every decision you make about content, and will ultimately be what helps you grab attention and direct it to your business.

Who Are You Creating Content For?

You might have heard the term "blogger" to describe people who create online content. "Blogger" became the term of choice when blogs were first introduced as a way for people to share their thoughts online. While content marketing as an idea has been around for hundreds of years, the focus on *online* content has thrust the content marketing concept onto a new level.

A blogger is someone who creates content on a blog. As I've mentioned already, your job is not primarily about creating content. Your job first and foremost is about marketing a business *with* content. That's why I prefer the term "content marketer," and the focus for content marketers is, therefore, the business.

I want you to think of yourself as a content marketer.

You're someone who has a business, wants to grow their business, and wants to use content to do it. When you create your content it has to be targeted, because the ultimate goal is to sign up customers. That doesn't mean you expect customers to convert directly from your blog posts. That is very unlikely, particularly early on. Content marketing is a long-term strategy, not a direct response marketing technique.

However, how *well* your content is targeted is critical.

There is an undercurrent that flows through all of your content, and that is your customer. These customers are part of communities that your content has to appeal to.

If Dave Asprey's or Tim Ferriss's businesses were aimed at conservative senior executives, their experimental ways would fall on deaf ears.

There are two ways to define who you are creating content for. One is to come up with a "Customer Avatar" that describes exactly who your ideal customer is, what their wants and needs are, and what they are looking for in your content.

For example, let's say we define a person: John, who is a 32-year-old male entrepreneur struggling to create an eye-catching site and grow his business.

The accepted wisdom around avatars suggests that you would create a piece of content for John; he would find it through Google, having never heard about your company before; and then he would sign up to be a customer because he trusts you.

The problem is, in my business and in most cases that I've seen, it rarely works that way.

That's why I think taking this avatar approach is the wrong way to go about it.

Here's a closer example of how it normally works. For WP Curve, our ideal customer is John. He's an established entrepreneur with a real business. He's not super passionate about WordPress, but he does use it for his site and wants it to be secure and valuable to his business.

- John watched a video by Bryan Harris on **Videofruit** (http://videofruit.com) about how Bryan is increasing email conversions with the help of WP Curve.
  We helped Bryan design the content idea for his audience. John isn't particularly interested in email conversions, but he loves Bryan's videos.
- John attends the WordPress conference WordCamp, because his hosting company is sponsoring the

event. I'm speaking at the event on how to build a WordPress business, and John attends the talk. He's in business himself, so he finds the topic interesting.

- Two months later, John starts to think about how he can improve his own site, and when he catches up with a fellow entrepreneur, Brooke, over coffee, she mentions she just listened to a WordPress episode on Pat Flynn's **Smart Passive Income** (http://www.smartpassiveincome.com/) podcast. It was with a guy named Dan from WP Curve, who discussed how to improve WordPress sites. He checks out our site and remembers that he saw me talk at WordCamp.
- A month later he asks his developer to install a new SEO plugin, and his site crashes. It's late at night and his developer is MIA. He googles "WP Curve", jumps on the live chat, and signs up.

This is typically how content marketing works. Some of our customers had been following my content for five years before they signed up. It doesn't work the same way for everyone.

This indirect relationship between content and a sale means the typical advice, "Choose an avatar and create for them," doesn't really work. Your ideal customers will hear about you over a long period of time, through multiple sources, and that is how trust is built.

A better way to think about it—and the second way to define who you are creating content for—is to choose a community and help them with what they need.

Some people in the community might end up becoming a customer. They might fit your profile directly. Most, however, will simply become consumers and advocates of your content. Some may just read it and occasionally engage with it (comment or share). Others might become raving fans and share it with everyone they know. These are all good results, because they get your brand in front of more people through more sources.

In the examples above, if we had created some content called "How to fix SEO plugin theme crashes", we would not land John as a customer. Why?

Well, to start, we wouldn't have created the video with Bryan on his site, Videofruit, because we were too busy creating content for John, and John doesn't care about email conversions.

I would never have presented at WordCamp, because WordCamp is for passionate WordPress geeks like myself, not for busy entrepreneurs like our ideal avatar.

Brooke would never had heard my podcast with Pat Flynn, because I never would have done it. I know more traditional entrepreneurs like John don't listen to Smart Passive Income. It's for the younger, modern-tech-savvy crowd.

Instead, our strategy is to help out web-savvy entrepreneurs with their business and online marketing. While this is a broad strategy based on an ideal community rather than an avatar, it's extremely beneficial.

It means when Bryan asks for help with doing a piece on his site, we say yes. When WordCamp asks me to present, I say yes. When Pat Flynn asks me to be on his podcast, I say yes. It results in free, useful content for our community, and, in the long term, it builds trust and spreads the word of our brand.

I have no expectation that any of it will lead to direct sales, and it rarely does. But it's a content marketing strategy that works over time.

Don't be picky about whether each piece of content is generating leads. Just create as much value as you can for the most amount of people in your chosen community. Give away as many useful things as you can, create content that people can really relate to, and if possible, offer a unique perspective that people haven't come across before.

Who is your community?

How are you going to help them?

Spend a good amount of time thinking about this and have it documented in your content strategy.

Onsite vs Offsite: The 70/30 Rule

Since you are creating content for a community, it's important that you get in front of those community members. For people starting out with content marketing, I like the idea of the 70/30 rule. When you have an established content marketing machine, you have a big enough audience for posts to gain traction on their own. If you're starting out, however, you don't have this luxury, so you need to focus on getting new people into your audience. The last thing we want is for you to create a whole bunch of content, get no traction, and have your motivation suffer.

The 70/30 rule says that when you still don't have a big enough audience for your posts to gain traction on their own, focus 70% of your efforts on off-site content. This could include guest posting, content partnerships, interviews on other podcasts, or more actively promoting your content. The remaining 30% should be spent on on-site content.

Once you have your audience, you can flip it the other way and do 70% on your own site and 30% off-site. As you get a more established audience you might find the off-site content portion goes down even further, but probably never stops completely (even the content godfather **Seth Godin** [http://www.sethgodin.com/] turns up on other people's podcasts every now and then).

The point is: you need to get new people seeing your content, because your small existing audience won't do enough sharing to get your name out there.

So write some guest posts, go on some podcasts, and talk to other influential people in your niche about doing some co-authored content to increase the "new" traffic on your site.

That's The Basics—Now What?

As you know, it took me a long time to get content marketing right. I'm confident, with the lessons in this book, that you can do it much quicker than I did.

You've confirmed that your business either has the 10 Characteristics of a High-Growth Business, or you are working on building a business that aspires to have them. You've taken some time to sit down and write out your 10-Minute Content Strategy, and given some serious consideration to your vision and who you are creating content for.

You have accepted that you will have to take the leap of faith, because it's unlikely that you will get outstanding short-term results with content marketing. But you have a trick up your sleeve. Create most of your content offsite to start with to get some early attention and traction.

In the next chapter, we are going to jump into the fun stuff: how to create high-quality content that people care about.

CHAPTER 3

HIGH QUALITY CONTENT

Now that you have a good foundation in business and understand the basics of content marketing, you are ready to work on figuring out how to create content that people care about.

Not all content is equal.

You don't get rewarded for the amount you produce. You could write thousands of low-impact posts and get virtually zero benefit. On the other hand, I've seen people make a name for themselves and their brand with just a handful of high-impact posts.

I want you to think of yourself as a designer and a creator, not a robot. Quantity doesn't matter. Impact matters. In this chapter I want to show you how to create high-impact content that people care about.

Let's Start Creating Some High-Quality Content

If your content is not high quality, it won't grab people's attention, and your business won't get the benefit it deserves. Other than fundamentally broken or non-existent businesses, poor-quality content is the other top reason content marketing fails.

I'm constantly amazed at how many people (including content marketing experts), simply don't "get" what great content is. Luckily for you, this won't be a problem once you finish this book.

Here's my definition:

Great content is something you provide to your audience that captures their attention and encourages them to engage and share.

The two parts of that sentence will form the basis of your content marketing from here on in:

1. Great content succeeds when people engage with, comment on, and share it. Just creating *lots* of content isn't good enough. Getting lots of pageviews isn't enough. If people aren't truly engaging with it in a meaningful way, then it's not great content.
2. Great content needs to capture attention. That means it's tightly related to how good your competitors are at vying for your audience's attention. For example,

> a blog post on "How to drive sideways" is not going to compete with Red Bull's WRX video[1] that shows a professional driver going sideways down a public street in San Francisco. But if your competitor is publishing *no* content, then your article will be mighty effective. This is a theme throughout the book. Content marketing is generally like business. There is no blueprint for content marketing success—there is only doing something better than your competitors.

When people come to me and tell me they aren't getting traction on their content, it's almost always because it's not great content. It's broad instead of highly specific and actionable; it's the same generic info and nothing new or unique; and it's boring. People don't love it, they don't engage with it, they don't share it, and you have competitors creating content that is better.

It is literally that simple.

No amount of poor content is going to get you the results you want.

Lessons Learned From Bad And Good Content

Since poor quality is one of the top causes of failed content, there is one question you have to keep coming back to: Is my content actually good?

As you know, I did hundreds of pieces of content before I got any traction. In the end I had to accept that it was because the content wasn't good enough.

Through years of trial and error and asking myself the above question, I eventually arrived at these seven lessons, which I keep coming back to. These things have consistently resulted in high-impact content that has reached traction and broke me out of my bad rut.

If one of these resonates with you, think about how you can add them to your strategy and use them when you generate ideas.

1. Don't Be Afraid To Go Outside Your Niche

Content must not be boring. If you are in a boring niche, don't feel like you need to create content around topics in your niche. Think more about your community and what they care about.

For example, if you have a backup company, you may not have much success with posts about why people should back up their files. People don't get excited about that. Think about who your ideal community member is and what other things they *do* get excited about, and create content about those things.

Maybe your ideal customer is a location independent entrepreneur who needs to have their files centrally backed up. Why not inspire them with stories of other entrepreneurs travelling the world? That will be more interesting, and when they think about backups, they'll think about you.

Remember our definition of content marketing? If it's not interesting, it's not content marketing.

Creating niche-specific content is the easy option, and it will be the first thing your competitors do. Get the jump on them by going outside this content to more interesting topics.

2. Care About Your Community

If you create a deep connection with your community, they will become a never-ending source of topic ideas. I will talk more about building a community later. For now, have them in the front of your mind as you start to think about topic ideas.

Ask them what their problems are and what they need help with. Ask them what other sites they like and pay attention to what they share.

3. Be More Generous

Content marketing is a trust-building exercise, so the more generosity the better. In the next chapter, I will tell you about how I was inspired by Noah Kagan's appearance on the Smart Passive Income Podcast.

His generosity really took me aback, so I asked myself, "How can I be even more generous than that?" Noah had 650 comments on Pat's blog after that episode. How could I beat that?

I volunteered to review websites for anyone who posted a comment on the episode. At the time of writing, there are over 700 comments. I reviewed sites from all over the world, at airports and hotels as I travelled. I probably spent a full week in the comments on that site reviewing websites. What can you do to be more generous than your competition?

4. Be More Transparent

Being transparent is a natural trust builder. Transparency in business has become a trend of late, and it's a trend I have been very keen to embrace. I've released income reports since 2012 when I had no income. We've put all of our key processes up online, even the ones we use to hire our development team. I'm 100% open and honest about what is going on in our business in interviews and my writing.

You may not be comfortable taking this approach, and that is up to you. But it's something that I know works.

5. Be More Contrarian

It's not easy to get noticed among all the noise of the modern web. In the early days of blogging, it might have been okay to create some generic content and preach well-accepted maxims in your industry.

Now, you need something about your content that acts as a talking point. A point of difference or something that surprises people. People need to be given a reason to pay attention.

I wrote my first book, *The 7 Day Startup*, at a time when *The Lean Startup* was all the rage, and every entrepreneur was singing the praise of "validation". It started with a blog post I wrote called, "Is Startup Validation Bullshit?" It was my most successful blog post, and it convinced me there was an appetite for a book.

I put forward a contrarian view on validation, suggesting that for most self-funded founders it was a flawed exercise, and the only way to validate a startup was to launch it.

The 7 Day Startup went on to sell tens of thousands of copies and even briefly passed *The Lean Startup* in the Amazon rankings.

Offering a contrarian view got me a lot of attention. At the time of release the only startup book outranking it on Amazon was *Zero To One*, a book about how to build a business by being contrarian.

It's not essential that all of your content disagrees with everyone. It's just one way to get noticed, and every industry is filled with popular ideas that are ready to be tested as time goes on. Perhaps those well-held ideas just aren't relevant anymore?

Keep an eye out for this when you listen to podcast interviews or read articles in your industry. Thought leaders like Tony Robbins and Seth Godin use this technique all the time. "Most people think X, but actually…" If you are one of the people that think X, then you certainly need to pay attention to why Tony thinks you are wrong.

6. Be More Actionable

Challenge yourself to truly help people out and take action.

It's one thing to create something that is interesting, but it's another to create something that is truly useful. Useful, by definition, means that someone can take what you have produced and use it in their life.

For example, a list of top ten mistakes to avoid when writing a sales letter is interesting. An actual sales letter template which walks people through how to structure their own sales letter is truly actionable, because people can take it and use it.

That's why I've included lots of frameworks in this book. The book itself might be interesting, but I want you to take action on the information. The frameworks enable you to do that.

You can easily determine if something is actionable by looking at what people say about it. That could be in the comments on your site, on social media, or in reply to your emails. Are people saying things like, "Great post," or are they saying, "This is awesome! I've just set up X and I've used this post as a guideline"?

If you can create content that is legitimately actionable, it will get consumed more, shared more, and it will convert more readers to active community members or eventually customers.

Think about how people will use your content and what you can do to make it more likely that they will actually use it.

7. Tell A Better Story

The most powerful content in the world moves people in one way or another. It could be through humor, through surprise or shock, or just purely joy (entertainment). In short, you do it by telling good stories.

Storytelling is a great way to capture and hold people's attention. It's been proven over generations and is a simple strategy for you to use with your content. Learning how to craft stories and how to follow a framework to tell your story is a worthy exercise.

Have a look at this line chart that represents the story of Cinderella as designed by Kurt Vonnegut.[2]

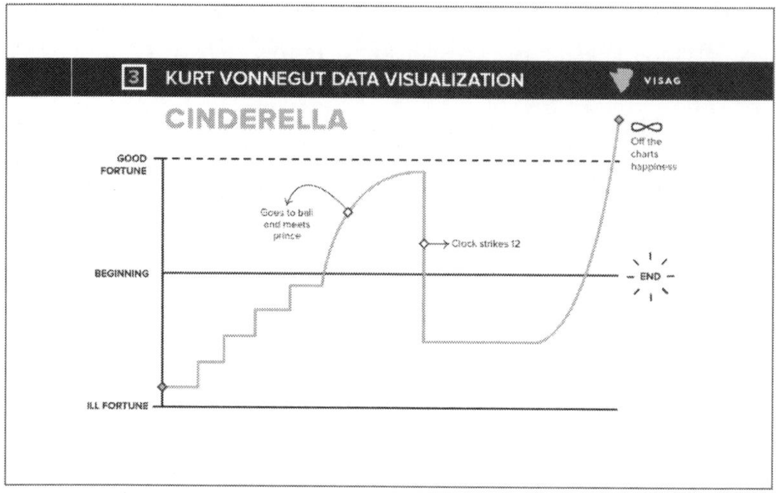

Look familiar?

Do you recall my income line chart from the beginning of this book?

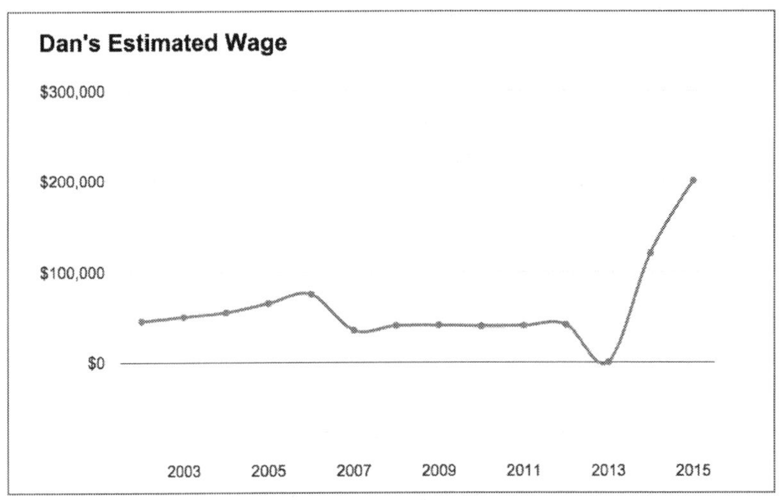

I tell my story like this often because people can relate to a story that follows this pattern of fortune and misfortune. They've learned to do so through years of books, movies, and stories passed down through generations. They relate to stories presented in this way on a deep subconscious level.

One of the best indicators that you are doing this is through feedback from people saying things like, "I feel like you wrote this about me," or "I'm exactly where you were and it's refreshing to see your progress." This comes down to knowing who you are creating content for (your community) and what they care about. Look out for people saying these things, and you will know you are on track.

Learn about storytelling models that would work for your topic areas and figure out a way to tell your story in a way that people can relate to.

Generating Your First 100 Content Ideas

In chapter two, Content Marketing Basics, we went over a content marketing strategy that included your vision and who you are creating content for. Now you can get to the fun part! What are you going to create content about?

I've found the most effective way to come up with content ideas is to use a proven framework for both generating topics and transforming those topics into content ideas. These are handy when coming up with a bunch of initial content ideas. After the first few you really start to get a feel for what your audience wants and ideas start coming to you from all angles.

This is where you want to be: a point where you aren't wondering what to create content on. This will come once you get traction. These idea frameworks will be useful if you aren't at this point yet or as a resource to return to if you do happen to run out of content ideas down the line.

Generating Content Topics (The Twenty Topics Framework)

Let's start with finding topics. These are the broad areas you will cover in your content.

I've compiled a list of about twenty ways you can find content topics. Even if you only find one through each item on the list, that will be enough to develop those into at least 100 pieces of content.

This framework is available as a downloadable resource at http://contentmachine.com/resources. It's a Google Doc that you can use to build a list of your own ideas.

1. **Twitter** (http://twitter.com) – Enter a keyword that represents your business, put a # in front of it (e.g. #wordpress, #startups, #onlinemarketing), and see what people are discussing. Pick a broad topic that sounds like a good fit.
2. **Google Analytics** (http://google.com/analytics) – Click on "Behaviour/Site Content/All pages". Make sure you have a decent time period selected, and you will get a good feel for your most popular content. Pick a topic that relates to content you have created successfully in the past. This obviously only works if you have already created content on your site.
3. **Google Webmaster Tools** (https://www.google.com/webmasters/) – Click on your site, click "Search traffic", and then click "Search Queries". This will list your top keywords. Choose the keyword that seems like the best fit for your blog. Again, this only works if you have already created some content.
4. **Meetup** (http://meetup.com) – Search for a broad keyword ("WordPress" or "Startups", for example) and see what sort of topics people are meeting up

about. If something catches your eye, add that as a broad topic to your list.

5. **Ask Your Audience** – Use your email sequence (I'll go over this chapter five if you don't have an email sequence set up yet), blog posts, or social media to ask people what they would like to hear your opinion on. One really simple way to do this is to have an automated email sent to people when they first sign up to your list that asks them what topic they are most interested in learning about.
6. **Guest Authors** – Look through blogs from others in the industry and find articles written by freelance writers. Get in contact with them and ask if they have any ideas about what to create for your site.
7. **Personal Story** – People love stories and everyone has a unique one. If you have a story that you think would help your audience, make sure you tell that on your site. It could be your personal story, a story from a team member, your business founding story, or customer stories.
8. **Help Desk** – If you have a support desk or enquiries email box, log in and have a look at the common things people email about. If people are often asking the same questions, it could be a good indication that it's a common problem you can help solve with some useful content.
9. **Trends** (http://google.com/trends) – Put in some broad keywords. Scroll to the bottom right for

additional keywords and see if you can tap into some hot topic areas.

10. **Inbox** – Open your inbox and look for emails from customers to find common questions. Replies to your autoresponder emails will be a great source of ideas. Just make sure you aren't using a no-reply email box and remember to specifically ask people to reply with ideas.
11. **Google AdWords Keyword Planner** (https://adwords.google.com/KeywordPlanner) – Click "Search for new keywords and ad group ideas". Enter some broad keywords and click "Get ideas". Look at the ad group ideas and the keyword ideas to find a few topics to cover.
12. **Forums/Groups** – Use forums or social media groups in your industry to see what people are discussing. Groups exist on Facebook, LinkedIn, and Google+, and it's never hard to find forums for most topics online.
13. **Competitors** – Visit your competitors' sites to see what posts are doing well. Some blogs have a "top posts" sidebar widget, and you can also look at the number of tweets for articles.
14. **BuzzSumo** (http://buzzsumo.com) – Search for broad keywords. It will list high traction articles from top blogs and give you more ideas for other topics.

15. **Top Industry Blogs** – Visit top industry blogs and see what they are covering. They often have a decent team who can find great topics to cover. You can offer a different spin on the same topics.
16. **Thought Leaders** – Use Twitter to search for industry thought leaders and see what they are sharing. You can simply search for keywords or one or two influential people you already know of, and Twitter will point you to other people to follow. Most influential people on Twitter are good at sharing the important content from their industry, which will be an easy way for you to see the popular topic areas.
17. **Amazon** (http://Amazon.com) – Look at the topics of popular books in a broad category relating to your industry. You can also read through the comments people are making about a certain book to learn what people are interested in.
18. **Quora** (http://quora.com) – Enter a few broad keywords into the search option. It will specifically list questions people have, along with the answers if they have been provided. This can be useful for a general topic and can also be a good source of quotes or answers for the content itself.
19. **Reddit** (http://reddit.com) – Find a subreddit for your niche and look at the trending threads. There is a subreddit for almost every topic you can think of, and they are often quite active. Most of

the time, Redditors are constantly sharing useful content from around the web.

20. **Podcasts** – Search iTunes for popular podcasts in your niche. Look through the episode titles and listen to some of the more popular episodes. This will show you some great general topic areas and also help you identify the influencers worth getting input from on your content.

Going through this process should result in at least twenty different broad topic ideas. If you are going through it for the first time, it could result in hundreds!

The next step is turning these topic ideas into actual pieces of content.

Creating Content Ideas (The Content Multiplier Framework)

Now that you have (at least) twenty different broad topic ideas, it's time to turn them into workable ideas for content.

To aid you in this step, I've put together the Content Multiplier Framework.

This framework is available as a downloadable resource at http://contentmachine.com/resources as a Google Doc. You can keep reusing it to come up with multiple content ideas. Here's how it works:

For every broad topic area, you can use the framework to multiply it into nearly a dozen ideas for content. I recommend just doing five to ensure that you only execute on the highest quality ideas.

Step 1 – Write Your Topic

Choose your first topic from the previous step. I would always start with the best topic possible to make sure I'm executing only the highest quality content. For this example, I'll choose the topic "WordPress speed", because that is our most popular blog post.

Step 2 – Write A Problem And Aspiration For The Topic

People are drawn to content that solves their problems or appeals to their aspirations. Take your topic and write out both a problem and an aspiration relating to the topic.

In my case, I've gone with:

- Problem: Having a slow site will escalate bounce rate and result in losing customers to your competitors.
- Aspiration: I want a site that runs as fast as WordPress.com.

Step 3 – Choose Up To Five Content Types

There are almost endless types of content you could potentially run with on your site. I've listed eleven common content types below. The idea here is for you to choose five that best represent the topic. I've bolded the ones I would want to choose for the WordPress speed topic.

1. **Case Study**
2. Guide
3. **Roundup**
4. How to
5. **How not to**
6. **Infographic**
7. Comparison/Review
8. Cost/Price
9. Data Driven
10. Best of/List
11. **Opinion**

I could have picked most of the options above, but I generally choose ones I think will come to me naturally, and those that would be unique compared to other solutions out there.

Step 4 – Brainstorm A Descriptive Title

In this step you will create a descriptive title for the content. For now, just make it a simple description of what the post is about.

Title 1 – How WP Curve reduced their bounce rate by 30%.

Title 2 – The ultimate guide for speeding up your site [INFOGRAPHIC].

Title 3 – Four experts weigh in on WordPress speed.

Title 4 – Six plugins that will slow down your site.

Title 5 – Things worth doing to speed up your site.

Step 5 – Add A Hook

In some cases you might leave the title as is, but if you can, add a hook to grab your reader's attention. It will have a *much* bigger impact. Always remember not to be too "over the top" with your hooks, or you will run the risk of disappointing your readers once they check out your content.

There are six hooks I've included in the framework for grabbing people's attention:

1. Contrarian – give them information that is the opposite of convention.
2. Surprising – give them a fact that will surprise them, something simple that is the opposite of what they might assume.
3. Overcome Objections – consider what their objections might be and directly respond to them in the title.
4. Guarantee – Give them a guarantee of success.

5. Interest – Give them interesting facts to chew on. Percentages or real world examples could work well.
6. Fear – Appeal to their inbuilt sense of fear.

Here are some examples from my topics above:

Title 1 – How WP Curve increased conversions and reduced bounce rate by 30% without compromising site quality.

The conventional wisdom might be that you have to make compromises to speed up your site.

Title 2 – The ultimate guide for making your site load faster than WordPress.com.

This would appeal to their aspirations and offer them the cool benefit of having a site loading faster than WordPress itself.

Title 3 – Matt Mullenweg and three other experts weigh in on their top ideas for speeding up WordPress.

This mentions a specific influencer which will grab their attention if they know WordPress (Matt created WordPress).

Title 4 – Five web design compromises worth making to speed up your WordPress site.

This is an opinion piece where I'd talk about the level of compromise that is worthwhile when it comes to speed.

Title 5 – How to avoid the average 20% reduction in conversions that result from slow websites.

This provides an interesting stat that could grab their attention.

Title 6– Six plugins that kill site speed (hint, you are probably using at least one).

This appeals to their sense of fear in thinking that they are making a big mistake.

Writing titles is a bit of an art form. If you want extra help with this, visit http://contentmachine.com/resources and check out the guide there on writing effective headlines.

Another useful habit is paying close attention to content that does really well in your niche. (BuzzSumo is great for this.) When you see the types of posts that are doing well, you will notice that their subject lines are often very well written.

Managing Content Ideas With A Content Calendar

I've found the easiest way to manage content ideas is using the free app, Trello. Trello is like post-it notes, but on the web. You can create a card for each idea, assign it to a writer, add notes, and much more. It even has an editorial calendar feature.

In chapter five, I'll talk more about how to use Trello, but for now it's worth setting up a free account and starting a "Content Marketing Ideas" board.

I've create a simple template board you can use, which you can grab at http://contentmachine.com/resources.

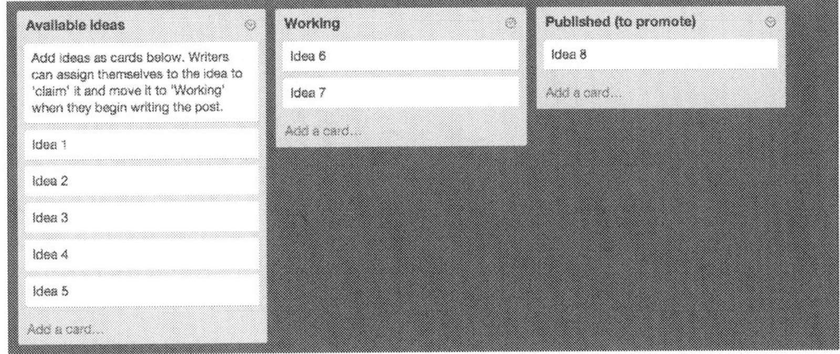

Understand And Leverage Your Strengths

I've mentioned that it took me a long, long time to find my way with content marketing.

Part of the reason is because I kept seeing other people succeeding in something, so I thought I'd try it as well.

With content specifically, and in business generally, this is a bad idea. Rarely have I been able to replicate someone else's success, because there are just too many variables.

Every content creator is unique, every audience is unique, every business is unique. Not to mention it's always hard to figure out why a person is actually successful. Often they don't have a good handle on it themselves!

What works for me is to experiment with what resonates with my audience, what I can do well, and what I can do consistently.

I tried out video, but I found I couldn't really do it at a high standard. I also found it stressful and hard to come up with ideas. Plus it got very little traction. I know it works well for some other people, but I don't like it, so I don't do it.

I've created a few podcasts over the years and recorded around 100 episodes of my own podcasts. However, I found it annoying to line up guests, and I couldn't find a unique angle for our podcast. It just felt like I was doing "yet another interview". On top of that, when it came to hiring a content marketing manager, it was a very difficult content type to delegate to someone else. For that reason, with WP Curve, I decided to only do guest interviews on other podcasts and not have our own.

If you are going to create content as a significant part of your day, you have to do it in a way that you love. One of the most common questions I get asked is: how do you find time? The answer is that I never really think about it. I don't have to find time. I do content, because I love doing it.

I'm writing this book on a plane. The guy next to me is watching a movie (hopefully he's not reading this). The guy in front is listening to music. The people behind me are sleeping. It's lunchtime on a Monday, but I don't want to be watching movies, listening to music, or sleeping—I want to be writing. So, I'm writing.

You might not like writing, which is cool. What do you like? Do you like presenting? That's an awesome way to create content, and you can easily have someone re-purpose it into videos for your website. Do you like talking to other entrepreneurs? If so, a podcast might be worth a go, or you can start doing free "office hours" calls and upload the transcripts to your website.

Maybe you like making videos, or designing, or coding. Whatever you enjoy, if you can point yourself in a direction that creates something useful for your community, then you are well on your way to creating good content.

If you are a designer and love designing things, don't write about design. Create logos and themes and give them away for free.

If you like presenting, record videos for YouTube or Instagram or stream content live on Periscope.

If you are a developer, create some plugins and give them away on your site. That's a great way to generate signups and shares.

You won't have to worry about "finding time" if you focus your efforts on things you love doing, particularly once you start getting rewarded for your work with a grateful community and a growing business.

Of course this assumes you have built a great business that enables you to spend time on what you love. If you are struggling with time, it could be worth revisiting chapter one.

Pay attention over time to what you love and what you can do well. Focus on that, and you will be in a good place.

Content Quality Standards

The other thing I've found useful is to set some high standards around making my content high quality. They may not be the same for you, so they aren't concrete rules—just personal observations.

You can use these as a starting point and adjust them to build your own list of high-quality content standards. You can even build them into your content creation guidelines, to ensure you and any guest contributors, remember them when it comes time to create content. A fair amount of this list would likely be applicable to most types of written content, particularly in the B2B small business space that I'm in.

This list is available as a download at http://contentmachine.com/resources as a Google Doc, so you can use it or customize it to your personal needs.

Useful

Would someone actually use this? Write to solve an issue or pain point for a community of people. If you are using these standards to review an existing piece of content, what can you do to make the content more useful?

Easy To Read

Ensure that your audience doesn't struggle to read your content. Have short intros, simple language, lots of white space, and eliminate fluffy language. Don't let pop-ups or other objects intrude on the writing. Readers like to skim through and hit all the high points quickly, so use bulleted points and lists; large, high-contrast text; clean images; and a minimalist, simple design to effectively hold their attention and make them want to return for more.

Has Credibility

Extra credibility helps. How else can you add credibility to this content? If the author has credibility to start with, that is great. Having opinions from experts included in the article is another way. Data and links from external sources is another way. Great design and high-quality writing is another.

Emotionally Relatable

If you are specifically targeting a community of people, you should have a good handle on who they are, what they feel, what challenges them, etc. Write stories that will appeal to their emotions. What images and words can you use that will grab them?

It's Not All About You

Some content about you can work well, but generally it should be about the reader. Look for more "you's" than "I's". The exception would be if you are specifically telling a personal story that you hope they can relate to.

Be Specific, Not General

Broad, general content is rarely useful. Be as specific as you can and use active language. A useful tool for finding sections where you use passive voice is the **Hemmingway Editor** (http://www.hemingwayapp.com/).

Be Generous

Look at your content and make a call on its motives. Are you just trying to get people to pay for something else? Or are you being legitimately generous?

Be Original

Is it a new idea or rehashed old stuff that has been said

thousands of times? Can you add something to the content to turn it into something that hasn't been done before?

Make It Shareable

Create the type of content people would share and tell others about. The way I think about it is, if 100 people just click "Like" on my content, that's 100 people who thought it wasn't good enough to share. It sounds harsh, but it's a good benchmark for quality.

Interesting

Remember, if it's not interesting, it's not content marketing. Is the headline eye-catching? Does the content have a good hook to get people in? Does the content itself have a unique perspective that will be interesting to your community?

High-Quality Design

Make sure your content is executed to a high standard design-wise. Does it have high-quality, original supporting images—not cheesy, pixelated stock photos?

Flow

Does the content follow a logical structure that draws readers from one section to the next? It should be easy to read from section to section. Include short intros and conclusions to sections or bridges to get people from one section to another.

Entertaining

If you can get a laugh in, that's a big bonus. Obviously, it's not always possible or desirable depending on the context. I talk more about humor specifically in chapter four.

Long

I have found that long and detailed content works well. Content posted on social media can (and sometimes must) be short, but if it's on your site, give the visitor something to sink their teeth into. Would readers bookmark it and come back to it when they need to implement the advice?

Monitoring Traction

Of course, just paying attention to what you want isn't a recipe for success. In the end, it's your audience that matters. You need to look at what content is resonating with them and find the sweet spot between what you are good at and what the audience loves.

Look at how your current content is performing. That's the easiest method. After 600+ posts, I arrived at a place where I knew the type of content that worked well for our audience. I did that by ignoring traditional metrics in favor of other, more meaningful ones.

A lot of people look at the number of views on an article to work out if it's successful. Views are relevant for media companies who sell ads based on the number of pageviews. For the rest of us, they don't tell us much about how much people care about our content.

People look at "Likes" and assume a lot of likes on a piece of content makes it good content. To me, a "Like" is a sign that the content wasn't good enough to share. They are setting the benchmark too low.

I recommend paying attention to three key metrics.

Shares

Rather than focusing on visits or likes, I suggest looking at social media shares. For our content specifically, I evaluate our Twitter stats. This gives me a good indication of what content is more likely to be shared. Someone reading it or "liking" it is great, but actually sharing is a whole new level. Only the best content gets shared. For our content, Tweets seems to be a more stable metric than LinkedIn or Facebook shares.

To work out total shares you can add buttons to your site or use **Like Explorer** (http://likeexplorer.com) or **BuzzSumo** (http://buzzsumo.com).

Comments

Much like shares, getting people to comment is another level above getting them to read or like a post. However, looking at the number of comments tends to be a bit of a vanity metric.

I recommend paying attention to the words people are using. I use a plugin called **Disqus** (https://disqus.com/), because I get higher quality comments with it (no spam or comments looking for backlinks). I found our income reports generated serious engagement and lots of interesting questions and advice from people. As a result, we ramped those up to a point where we do them every single month as the first piece of content we write.

I like to see evidence that people are getting real value out of content and actually taking action. Comments like "great post" are nice. But comments like, "This is really useful, I've applied this in my business," are far better. If people are actually using our content, we know it's effective.

Email Replies

We have an email list we've built up over the years, and each week we send out our best content. These come directly from my email address, and the replies tell me what is really resonating with people. Sometimes I'll get hardly any replies; other times, I'll be inundated with supportive messages or questions. That's when I know we've really nailed a piece of content.

Over time you will get a clear picture of what content works best for your audience. This will then feed back into your content strategy.

Sometimes the impact you have on people isn't easy to see. Cool, you got some tweets for an article—but do they care? Comments give you good insight into whether or not people care. Numbers don't matter, but the words people use do.

Content Driven SEO

To wrap up the chapter on high-quality content, we have to talk about SEO. Lots of people will tell you that when you are focusing on an effective content marketing strategy, you need to optimize everything to appeal to search engines. While I do agree that SEO is important, I think high-quality content is more important. When I think about SEO, I think about it mainly as a content quality issue.

I ignore the so-called "experts" who say they have a "secret" to ranking well in Google. In my experience, trying to outsmart Google is not the answer for long-term, sustainable traffic.

The right approach is much simpler than some sort of complicated SEO secret.

1. Don't Screw Up The Basic On-Page SEO Factors

Getting your website ready for SEO is very easy. In fact, if it's not ten years old, it's probably ready now. Here are the only four things you need:

1. Make sure your theme is using the right tags in the right places (for example, your post titles are H1 tags).
2. Make sure it's coded with clean HTML/CSS and not some old dodgy tables and other rubbish.
3. Make sure the URL of your content is logical. http://wpcurve.com/wordpress-speed is logical; http://wpcurve.com/p=45234dfg?? is not.
4. Make sure you are able to control the title, description, and URL of each post. If you are using WordPress, then the free plugin **WordPress SEO by Yoast** (https://wordpress.org/plugins/wordpress-seo/) does this.

2. Create Lots of High-Quality Content

Hopefully this chapter got you pretty fired you up to do this, but in case it didn't, know that Google loves lots of content. It doesn't love lots of *crappy* content, though. High-quality stuff is more to Google's taste. And it's smarter than you at determining what high-quality content is. So just trust me, and don't try to outsmart Google.

3. Do Basic Keyword Research When Needed

For a lot of my content, I don't target a specific keyword. I'd rather focus on the fundamentals, and if I have a good handle on my audience, then I can probably make a good decision on the sorts of keywords to target.

Sometimes, however, it makes sense to target a specific keyword, and it's not hard to quickly check Google to see what keywords are best to look at.

If you are just getting started with keyword research, the easiest option is the **Google Adwords Keyword Planner** (https://adwords.google.com/KeywordPlanner). I put in a broad keyword for what I want to write about, and then I'll choose a keyword that people are actually searching for. The tool enables you to filter by the number of exact searches. These numbers vary a lot depending on the authority of your blog. Early on you might want to choose a keyword with between 50 to 200 exact searches. Later on, it might be a few thousand. There are also more advanced keyword tools available if you want to delve further into the weeds on keyword research.

If you can spare the time, and you are working on a post that you think could be the best in your industry, choosing a popular keyword can be a wise move.

4. Optimize The Post For The Keyword

The final step is to optimize the post for your chosen keyword. Most website systems will enable you to do this. As I mentioned above, if you are using WordPress, this is where Yoast plugin comes in.

If you chose a specific keyword, that's cool; if you didn't, you can still do this step and just take a guess at what the dominant phrase might be in the content you've created. Yoast will give you a drop-down list of suitable choices once you start typing in the keyword idea.

To fully optimize the post, there are really only three main things you need to do.

1. Make sure your keyword is used in your post title. This, in turn, will ensure it appears in your heading tags, any auto generated internal links, and your page URL (permalink if using WordPress).
2. Mention the keyword in your first paragraph. Usually this is pretty easy, and you would do it anyway.
3. Make sure your SEO title (sometimes the same as your post title) includes your keyword and is the right length, and you have a description that includes your

keyword and entices the user to click through from Google. If you want to use a different SEO title, this can be easily done with a plugin like Yoast.

There are a lot more detailed optimization steps you can take, but these are the basics and they have served me well. Focusing on the absolute essentials might seem like a cavalier approach, but to me the quality of the content is more important than the optimization choices.

People share and link to high-quality content. This is what Google loves, and that will never change.

High-Quality Content? Check. What's next?

You've been through the fundamentals of high-quality content, part one of the three aspects to making content marketing work. But how do you create your content in a way that gets noticed and gets better results?

In the next chapter we'll run through some case studies of entrepreneurs who have done just that and provide you with some practical tools to enable *you* to do the same thing. Some of these sites are well-known, established sources of content, and others are brand new and much smaller in scale. At least one of them should get you thinking about what you can use to differentiate your own content.

Notes

1. "DC SHOES: KEN BLOCK'S GYMKHANA FIVE: ULTIMATE URBAN PLAYGROUND; SAN FRANCISCO," Youtube video, posted by DC Shoes, July 9, 2012, https://www.youtube.com/watch?v=LuDN2bCIyus.
2. French, Katy. Visage (blog). http://visage.co/. "Kurt Vonnegut Graphs the Shapes of Stories." Last Modified August 13, 2014. http://visage.co/kurt-vonnegut-shows-us-shapes-stories/

CHAPTER 4

DIFFERENTIATION

How To Be An Entrepreneurial Content Marketer

As I discussed in the introduction, one of the biggest mistakes that failed content marketers make is focusing on the output and not the strategy. A blogger creates blog posts. A content marketer markets a business.

You need to be entrepreneurial to be a great content marketer. Most people think that entrepreneurs look for gaps in markets and enter those gaps. I believe that the most successful ones go into existing markets with a unique offering.

My business, WP Curve, hasn't created a new innovation. It's taken an existing healthy market (people paying developers to fix their website) and put a unique spin on it (unlimited fixes 24/7 for a standard monthly fee).

Uber entered an existing, large, healthy market (transportation) and put a unique spin on it (cleaner, safer, cheaper, and they actually show up when called).

Airbnb entered an existing, large, healthy market (hotels/accommodation) and put a unique spin on it (individuals rent their houses, so customers get more for less).

For the most part, this is what entrepreneurs do. They enter into an existing space with something better and different enough to get noticed. It's also what the world's best content marketers do.

They don't simply create content. They create content for a certain community of people, and they do it *better* with a unique angle so they get noticed. Remember, you want the thing you do differently to be something your customers care enough about to talk about.

This aspect of differentiation is the biggest opportunity for content marketers, and it's barely talked about in other content marketing books and articles.

Throughout this chapter, you can see how other successful marketers have broken out of the "write every day" struggle and found a way to create high-quality content that grabs attention and builds trust. You will find at least one strategy that may resonate with you and one that can be disruptive in your industry. Some industries are far more advanced than others—even the simpler tactics here could be explosive in certain industries.

When you read through these stories, think about things you can bring to your own content. Can you use aspects of Marcus Sheridan's approach by creating problem-solving content that other people keep secret? Can you be like Noah Kagan and give and give until you can't possibly be any more helpful? Would your audience be interested in the transparent details of what is going on in your business?

If you generate ideas for content using the blueprints in this chapter, remember to add them to your Trello board.

The Whisperer

In 2008/2009, the U.S. economy was tanking. The fiberglass pool business was not a good business to be in. Marcus Sheridan's business, River Pools and Spas, was struggling. He could no longer afford to pay the advertising he'd always relied on to keep his business breaking even.

Content marketing had been around for a long time. But the web was relatively new and traditional industries were a fair way behind, so neither Marcus nor his competitors had a strong online presence. In those days, content marketing systems were rare and the standard website was a "brochure site".

Marcus saw an opportunity. He knew Google was exploding in popularity, and the way people searched for businesses like his was changing. He didn't have much time, either—he had to act quickly. He gathered his team together and delivered an inspiring speech akin to William Wallace's epic monologue in *Braveheart*.

He tasked the team to write down the top questions that prospective customers ask. Between everyone, with duplicates removed, they arrived at 100 questions. They were things like:

- How much does a pool cost?
- How long does it take to install a pool?
- What approvals do you need to install a pool?
- What is the difference between a fiberglass and an inground pool?

Marcus knew that if customers were asking these questions of his team, they were probably also putting it into Google. However, when he Googled, "How much does a pool cost?" he got the same generic fluff that he expected: "call for quote", "there are too many factors", "we can't be held liable for quotes", etc. Marcus knew people weren't expecting an exact quote, but giving a rough guess would at least help them move onto the next stage of their decision-making process.

He decided that he could be the guy to let those secrets out. After all, everyone in the industry knew the answers anyway—there was nothing to lose.

So he got the team to write out answers to all of these questions and started posting them on his blog. They wrote posts about how much a pool costs, how much a fiberglass pool costs, how much an inground pool costs, and so on.

He even pulled the key articles together into an ebook and provided this to his customers before they engaged his team. This worked as a pre-sales qualifier and made the sales process a lot smoother. Customers trusted him, because he was helping them from the start.

While he answered hundreds of questions on his site, he identified five of the key things that customers liked hearing about:

1. Cost/price articles
2. Problems articles
3. Vs./Comparison-based articles
4. Review-based articles
5. "Best of" articles

His examples of each are:

1. How Much Does a Fiberglass Pool Cost?
2. Top 5 Fiberglass Pool Problems and Solutions

3. Concrete vs. Fiberglass Pools vs. Vinyl Liner Pools: Which Is Better?
4. A Review of Barrier Reef Fiberglass Pools
5. Who Are the Best Swimming Pool Builders in Richmond Virginia?

Marcus' business went on to become a breakaway success. Instead of failing like a lot of similar businesses at the time, it continued to grow and became the number one fiberglass pool company in the U.S., turning over multiple millions of dollars a year. His site continued to grow as well, and it became the number one resource in the world for fiberglass swimming pools.

What Marcus did was nothing advanced, certainly by today's standards. But it was something that no one else was doing yet in his industry, and therefore he got noticed.

I believe there are industries in the world where this approach can still work—sectors where people are still secretive and no one has taken on the role of the whisperer, revealing the secrets to the public and letting them make up their own mind.

In fact, with my new craft beer-making business, Black Hops Brewing, we are doing exactly that. With a bunch of simple posts about how we make the beer, our plans to set up a brewery, and other similar "behind-the-scenes" knowledge topics, we managed to obtain some amazing results. In the first few months of the blog, we've been featured on all the main craft beer blogs and in local papers, and we've received four investment offers to build our own brewery. Every event we go to, we run into people who tell us they read the blog and love it.

This transparent approach to doing business, where you confidently give out secrets that others keep close to their chest, is a big trust builder. It's also a great way to tell your story and people love a good story.

How To Become A Whisperer

Step 1 – Research the most important "top five content" keywords for your field. For example, if you are a bookkeeper, you might use: "How much does a bookkeeper cost".

Step 2 – Visit Google and search for each keyword phrase, one at a time. Start to look through the results to see (a) if the same site keeps ranking for them, and (b) how good the content is on the topic. Ignore the paid ads—just look at the organic listings and use our previous criteria for good content to make a decision on the quality. In this case, it would likely be a utility that you would look for. If there are posts that skirt around the issue in a vague way, then there is a good opportunity for you to create something better.

When I started looking around for good content about starting a craft beer brewery, I only found one blog that had legitimately useful, real advice on costs, the process, etc. That blog had one or two older articles—other than that, the information was just not out there. If you find the same thing, that's a great result!

If you think there is a gap, you are ready to create the content.

1. Start with Marcus's top five customer questions and put them through the Content Multiplier framework available at http://contentmachine.com/resources. This will give you a bunch of potential articles for each one. For example, "How much does a bookkeeper cost" could become "How to avoid excessive bookkeeping fees", "6 simple steps to bookkeeping bliss", "A simple process used by X to reduce their bookkeeping costs", "The 3 most affordable bookkeeping tools reviewed", etc.
2. Take another leaf out of Marcus's book and look internally. Ask your team what the common questions are and ask them to write out solutions to those questions.
3. Create a post for each one of your content ideas. Review the Content Quality Standards to ensure that it is high-quality content.
4. Once you have exhausted Marcus' top five questions, look through the first twenty topics framework

for more sources of where you will find common problems and repeat the steps.

A few other notes about this strategy:

- Be personal with the content. This strategy is about building trust long-term. Write them under your own name, include your picture, and use casual (but not lazy) language. Customers love this and it makes them feel like they are talking directly with the owner of the business.
- Don't come at it from a position of disdain towards your competitors (e.g. "Our competitors will have you believe…"). Bagging out other people doesn't build trust. Take ownership of your role at educating your customers and accept that they will be the ones to judge whether they like you better than your competitors.
- Have your best content in an ebook or some sort of downloadable, behind-an-email opt in. This type of content works well via email, so after they opt in for the ebook, you can send out regular communications. As a result, when they are ready, you are top of mind. I go into more detail on this process in Scale: Building The Machine.
- Get active in the community, either on social media, in person, or in forums. This type of content is going to need a bit of a kickstart—you will have to put

> yourself out there as a helpful person to go to for information like this. This only really happens by *being* that helpful person. Over time people will recognize it; you can send them to the site, and ask them to share the content if it's useful. Gradually, Google will realize that your site is the authority on the topic.

Also, keep in mind that this isn't the most advanced content strategy. If it works for you, great. But stay on your toes and be ready to innovate if your competition catches up. This is an easy strategy for them to replicate.

The Hustler

Every once in a while, someone comes into a market and completely blows everyone out of the water. It doesn't happen that often, certainly not in the online marketing field where everything is tried and tested. But it happened in late 2012, when John Lee Dumas started **Entrepreneur on Fire** (http://www.entrepreneuronfire.com/).

A few months before, I'd been sitting in a presentation in the Philippines listening to how Dan Andrews turned his podcast, **Tropical MBA** (http://tropicalmba.com), into a successful business. One thing Dan mentioned was finding a unique angle, and he put forward the idea of a daily entrepreneurship podcast. I didn't think much of it. It honestly sounded like it would be too hard and altogether not very useful.

I guess everyone else thought the same thing. That is, everyone except John Lee Dumas.

John was busy working on exactly that: a daily podcast for entrepreneurs. It wasn't going to be all that different from other interview podcasts like Mixergy or This Week in Startups, except it would be daily. Every day, he would interview a new entrepreneur.

John started by working with an experienced marketer and podcaster, Jaime Tardy. He attended New Media Expo and, through Jaime, connected with a lot of big names in the space such as Derek Halpern and Pat Flynn. He asked them on the spot if they would come on his show. To his delight, most people said yes and then followed through as well.

Meanwhile, he told anyone who would listen about his great new idea. Most people came back with the same answers. "That's not possible", or "You can't do that many!", or "You'll run out of entrepreneurs", or "Do people even want to listen to a podcast everyday?", and, of course: "How are you going to make money? You have no business model."

John pushed on and started interviewing as many entrepreneurs as he could in the lead up to releasing the podcast. His idea was to stack up 30 or 40 interviews so he could hit the ground running when he launched. His other genius insight was to make sure the big name influencers were on the first few episodes. This gave him huge launch traction and immediate credibility.

John and his partner Kate did hit the ground running—and they kept running. They've built a seven-figure business off the back of their podcast in less than two years. They've interviewed over 1,000 entrepreneurs and released a podcast every day since they started. If that wasn't enough, Kate has even launched her own podcast!

I don't think John got there solely because of the unique angle he took. I'm still not convinced that having a podcast every day is a big factor in choosing a podcast to listen to. I think he just got there through pure hard work. He out-hustled everybody.

Everyone else was doing one podcast a week at best. John said, "Nope, I'll do ten podcasts in one day." On Mondays he stacks his interviews back to back and loads them up for the week. It's a big day, but then the rest of the week, he's free to work on his business and do other marketing like off-site podcast interviews and webinars. And because he does more than a week's worth at once, he can stack them up for when he takes a few weeks off.

He took it to a whole new level, and his initial burst onto the scene kicked off a ball of momentum that continues to roll forward to this day. He was featured in iTunes New and Noteworthy, getting great rankings from iTunes in his first eight weeks. He was mentioned consistently by the big influencers he had on the show during the first few weeks of launch. This gradually grew his listenership as people came in from all walks of entrepreneurship.

He has built on his content, releasing amazing monthly reports and useful webinars. He's developed strict processes around his content that has enabled him to execute his part in batches, and the rest happens without his involvement. Because his episodes keep coming out so regularly, the downloads keep going up, and other businesses are knocking down his door to advertise on his show. He makes over $60,000/month just in advertising through his podcast. This represents a fraction of his overall revenue, but it's not bad for one day's work per week!

I think there are certainly a lot of industries where people need to be blown out of the water. Where it's common to just write one general post per week, or create one video. Where someone can come in and burst onto the scene with pure hustle and ride the wave of momentum from there.

Is your industry like this?

How To Become A Hustler

Again, as with the "Whisperer" differentiator, this probably isn't going to work if someone is already doing it. If you are into entrepreneurship interviews, then you are out of luck.

You won't get the attention doing the same thing that John is already doing.

So have a look around to see what is going on in your industry. Look on Google to see what's ranking for content around your topic. Look on social media to see what articles people are sharing and how those people are going about creating their content. Look in iTunes and YouTube to see what the industry leaders are doing.

Here are a few things you might want to try:

- Release more content, perhaps a daily podcast or daily blog post.
- Release longer content. Perhaps the incumbents are releasing general, boring 500-word posts. Can you do 2,000-word detailed posts?
- Be more generous. What can you give away? Are others asking people to "sign up for emails"? Can you give away an ebook, some software, some processes, or frameworks? Can you do it without even asking for their email?
- Can you utilize new platforms? Check iTunes, Medium, YouTube, the App Store, iPad magazines, **Periscope** (https://www.periscope.tv/), **Snapchat** (https://www.snapchat.com/), Kindle—everywhere. Can you come into a platform and fill it with the best content and take that space away from incumbents who are focusing elsewhere?

There are also some logistical things you'd have to consider:

- Do you need to hire virtual assistants to help with the core part of the work?
- Can you hire someone to ghostwrite or guest write the content?
- Will you get your team to help?
- Will you utilize external services for part of the process or hire a remote team?
- What is your plan for when you are sick or you are away—can you stack the content up?

Ultimately, working out how it gets done in the long term is probably a problem you *can* solve (particularly if you have a budget). Short term, it might just be a case of working harder and longer than everyone else and sticking with it no matter what. That might be an unpopular message, but that's how John did it and that's the hustler's mentality.

If you are going to do the daily thing, you can create the posts in WordPress and use the scheduler to publish them in the future. A lot of the steps required to help with this level of content production can be managed by a Virtual Assistant for $400-$500 a month, full time. Check out **Virtual Staff Finder** (http://virtualstafffinder.com) if you want to go down this path.

The Giver

Noah Kagan is a guy I could have featured in a few of these chapters. Noah really shines in his approach to how much he gives away.

Ultimately, content marketing is about creating value for a community of people. The more you can give away, the more you are going to stand out. It's quite easy to give away a few small blog posts, but how far could you take it?

I first noticed the extreme nature of Noah's giver mentality on his interview[1] with Pat Flynn on Smart Passive Income. He talked about validation and starting new businesses. Not just his own story about how he started **AppSumo** (http://appsumo.com), but lots of practical advice on how other people could do the same.

It was one of the most useful podcast interviews I've ever listened to. But for Noah, that wasn't enough. After about an hour of straight value bombs when the interview was wrapping up, Noah asked, "What can I do to make this the best interview you've ever done?" When Pat responded, Noah kept going, rattling off more useful things for people to try.

But he still wasn't done. "You know what we should do?" he said. "I should have someone from your audience fly out to Austin, and they can spend the whole day with you and me working on their business." I knew Noah has charged $10,000 for a day of his time, but he was in giving mode, and nothing would stop him creating the most valuable interview on record on the show.

Since then, Noah has taken it to whole new levels again. His AppSumo business sends out giveaways on anything from ebooks to software tools. Well-known software tools like Neil Patel's Crazy Egg and others have provided lifetime free accounts to people in his audience. He started releasing his own plugins under the **SumoMe** (http://sumome.com) brand. At first a Twitter highlighter tool, then a heat maps tool, then a pop-up tool, then a content marketing analytics tool—all for free. All that on top of regular high-quality, detailed posts via his blog **OK Dork** (http://okdork.com), and regular appearances on podcasts and webinars to help other entrepreneurs.

Noah is a giving machine, and he has taken that approach to build an email list of close to one million people, a brand that is recognized by every entrepreneur I know, and a multi-million dollar business.

While other entrepreneurs were working on blog posts, he gave away software, training, his time, advice, plugins, and more.

How To Be A Giver

I would say that out of all of the differentiation strategies, this one is the most likely to work. And yet, even in the online marketing space, this approach is rare. Most people don't give away useful resources that people would happily pay for to such an extent. This is how we have grown a lot of our audience—with free books and plugins and giving away a lot of my time.

In more traditional industries, these opportunities are endless.

Have a look to see what others in your industry are doing. If you don't see all of the things on the list below, then get to work!

I wouldn't be afraid to spend money on giving away things. Just remember that even giving people free incentives creates expectations of support later on, and those have costs. It may be money well spent, but make sure to budget for ongoing support.

Here are a few things you might want to consider giving away. Keep in mind, it needs to be something valuable to your community.

- "Big content" books. Doing a free book on Amazon.com exposed me to a whole new audience that wouldn't have known about me or WP Curve otherwise.

- Organized, in-person events.
- An app that does something useful for your community.
- Onsite calculators or graders that make your community members' lives easier. These are often cheap to build and get a lot of interest.
- WordPress plugins or other small software items. People love free software!
- Your time, via office hours or doing an AMA (Ask Me Anything) thread in a forum, or being interviewed on podcasts. I do three to four of these per week, and I use **Schedule Once** (http://scheduleonce.com), so people can easily book times directly in my calendar.
- Industry guides that help everyone in the industry.
- Email courses on helpful topics.
- Video training on YouTube or sites like **Udemy** (https://www.udemy.com/).
- Conference presentations—perhaps you can present, sponsor, and make time for people to chat with you. Simply be more generous and give more than everyone else.

There's no shortage of what you can do here, and the only downside is that you will help others in the industry. It might cost you some time or money, but it's not time or money wasted as it is with advertising. It's helping someone, and in the end, it will probably come back around to help you.

The Analyst

Is it possible that, buried deep in the data of your business, there exists stories with the potential to go viral all over the world? Well, if you are in the business of dating like **OKCupid** (http://www.okcupid.com/), then the answer is a resounding yes.

Through analyzing the data gathered by the site, the team at OKCupid have been able to produce consistent viral content for their blog, building their business into a $50 million exit in the process. All of this in one of the most competitive niches in the world, which is littered with high-profile failed companies.

Take their "10 Charts About Sex". At the time of writing, the post has over a million views and 4,000 tweets.

Their style is quirky, somewhat controversial, but genuinely analytical. Perhaps an article about whether vegetarians are less or more likely to enjoy giving oral sex would be silly. But backed by data, and portrayed in a chart… well, that's just clever!

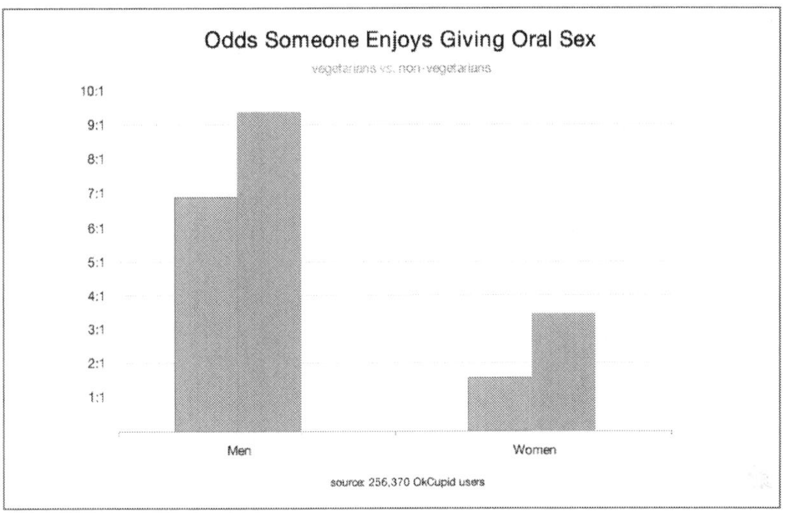

Gathering and reporting on original data is one of the best ways to build a content marketing strategy. Why? Because it's automatically differentiated. It's difficult, if not impossible, for competitors to report on the same data as you.

The Content Marketing Institute have a yearly report on what's going on in content marketing that they produce themselves. Each year they have guaranteed press, a bunch of sites linking to them and discussing the report, a whole suite of aesthetically pleasing brochures and presentations, and an open license to market their own institute by way of educating the public.

Some companies gather and report on data based on information they are already collecting. Some undertake dedicated surveys to produce unique content.

Analysing and reporting on data is a tried and true content marketing formula. As long as you have enough data to draw on, and the ability to create content that is unique, you have a good shot at making this work.

If you don't have enough data to draw on, research efforts like this are well suited to partnerships with other companies. Alternatively, you can simply survey a bunch of influencers. Every two years, Moz brings together over 100 SEO experts to pull together their **Moz Ranking Factors Report** (http://moz.com/search-ranking-factors).

How To Be An Analyst

Assuming you don't have the data in-house, an easy way to get started with this strategy is to undertake a basic group survey. Here is a quick summary of how to make it happen. In the process of writing this book, we did this internally at WP Curve, creating the Startups Content Marketing Survey with great results. You can see an example of our report at http://contentmachine.com/resources.

- Use a survey tool like **TypeForm** (http://www.typeform.com/) or **Google Forms** (http://www.google.com/forms/) to build and send out a survey. We used TypeForm, because it creates great-looking surveys and looks very professional.

- With the results, write up a well-designed graphical report which summarizes the results. If you don't have a designer in-house, Google Sheets is an easy way to build the charts.
- Create a SlideShare summary of the result for sharing and a full PDF report for your site.
- Write a press release and share it with journalists who would likely be interested in the topic.
- Use **Click to Tweet** (http://clicktotweet.com) to pull out the most effective tweets from the survey results and include them in the posts you write.
- Reach out to other blogs who cover the same sort of topics, and send them the report with some quotables to share with their audience. Give them the **SlideShare** (http://www.slideshare.net/) embed code as well, so they can embed it directly in their content.
- Reach out to influencers and ask for their opinion on the results. Ask them to share the report.

The cool thing about data collection and reporting is the whole industry benefits, so it's easy to get people behind the idea.

If you can create something useful for your industry, you can build processes around doing a survey like this every year.

The Comic

"What would Steve do?" asks Matt, the founder of **Vooza** (http://vooza.com/), walking confidently across the stage at the 2014 Next Web Conference.

"You need to emulate the young Steve Jobs." He pauses. "How do you do that?" His slides show a quick list of actionable steps.

1. *Wear a black turtleneck* (he's wearing one).
2. *Stop showering.*
3. *Take LSD as much as possible.*

The crowd erupts in laughter as Matt expected, and he moves on.

Matt is a comedian, so he knows simple comedy tricks like the Rule of Three (things that come in threes are funnier than other numbers of things).

Matt runs a fictional startup called Vooza. The company describes itself as "a mobile web app that steals data from your phone, so they can sell it to Eastern European spammers" after pivoting from "Spotify meets Grinder but for rental cars".

They originally launched through a series of videos talking about the (fake) product. Those videos got the attention of the startup world, which was held in suspense before Vooza announced what they actually did: created video content for startups, featuring native advertising.

Vooza are a team of professional stand-up comedians, and they have executed this idea well.

How To Be A Comedian

I debated whether or not to include this differentiator in the book, because being funny is not an easy task for non-comedians. In the end, I decided that even if you only remember one of these tips and make your content just one percent funnier, then you are better off. That is how powerful humor can be.

Even if you don't want humor to be your only thing, adding some humor into what you already do can be an epic way of getting attention. **Marie Forleo** (http://www.marieforleo.com/) is a great example. She has built a business education empire by delivering serious messages in a fun and quirky way.

Magically transforming your personality into Marie's isn't something you can (or should!) do. However, you can definitely add a bit of your own style of funny, and that might be enough to help you stand out.

So. Can you train yourself to be funny?

David Nihil, author of *Do You Talk Funny: 7 Comedy Habits to Become a Better (and Funnier) Public Speaker*, says yes.

David started off like the rest of us: petrified of public speaking. But he transformed himself into a professional stand-up comedian in a year-long experiment. He now runs a startup helping businesses use humour in their content. In fact, his business, **FunnyBizz** (http://funnybizz.co/), offers a service that specifically rewrites blogs posts and makes them funnier.

According to David, most stand-up comedians have become masters at a structured craft as opposed to being naturally funny people.

The rule of three, used by Matt above, is one example.

Incorporating some of the tricks used by stand-up comedians to generate more laughs can dramatically transform your otherwise boring content into an engaging, shareable piece that stands out from the crowd.

Here are some of David's tips:

1. Tell a story in a relatable way, include something broad that people can specifically relate to (maybe local references), then bring it back to something that happened to you.

2. Set the scene. Write as if you are describing something to a blind person, and be very specific with detail.
3. Use emotive or funny words like "weird", "crazy", or "nuts", and be passionate. Underpants is 15% funnier than underwear. Words with K in them are also considered funnier than others.
4. Use present tense—"I'm walking and I see" rather than "I was walking and I saw".
5. Use the rule of three to create memorable content. Build tension and surprise with items one and two and something unexpected with three.
6. Add a callback at the end to tie it together.

David says the safest humor involves personal stories, because they are guaranteed to be original and can be easily practiced and perfected. Often great stories come from seemingly mundane topics, and once you start telling stories you will find they really work. Even if you fail on the humour, your content will be more memorable.

My friend Kevin Rogers is an ex-stand-up comedian, and he's also a world renowned copywriter. He offers a specific structure for making stories funny:

1. Identity – Who are you; set the scene; who are you with; how are you feeling?
2. Struggle – What are you struggling with?
3. Discovery – What was your big discovery?

4. Surprise – What is a surprising twist that no one is expecting?

This is a structure used by comedians all the time to tell stories and jokes. The key is the "Surprise" component or where you "reframe" what the person thinks you are going to say.

As a content marketer you'll often find yourself telling stories. Even if you can include just a few of these tips in those stories, it might be enough to stand out from the crowd.

Kevin's free book, ***60-Second Sales Hook*** (http://60secondsaleshook.com), is a great place to start to dig into this further.

The Pioneer

In October 2008, Pat Flynn announced that he would write a blog post each month reporting on the income generated from his online marketing efforts.

These days, the idea of transparently reporting on your income is a growing trend. In 2008, however, this was highly unusual. There has always been a lot of hype and secrecy in the online marketing space, and Pat vowed to usher in a new era of transparency.

Pat created his site, **Smart Passive Income** (http://smartpassiveincome.com), and began writing monthly entries for how his various efforts were going. In that month he managed to bring in $7,900 from a few sources. Pat was laid off a week earlier, referred to his earnings as "a very successful month", and hoped he could continue with that revenue so he didn't have to get another job.

In the years since, Pat has become a household name in the online marketing space. His revenue is consistently ten times what it was in October 2008 and his income reports have formed the platform for a site that generates millions of visits each year. Pat is now an international speaker, author, software entrepreneur, and online celebrity. And no, he didn't have to get a job.

It's not *what* Pat did that was the difference—it was *when* he did it. These days, releasing your income online is a trend adopted by a lot of up-and-coming startups. WP Curve releases a monthly income report, and it's one of our most popular posts each month. Buffer, a company doing $4 million in revenue per year, releases their live company metrics, staff wages, investment data, and anything else you could imagine online.

But it's 2015. In 2008, it was unheard of and Pat Flynn was the pioneer.

For every trend in content marketing, there's one company at the forefront that creates a momentum burst to keep them going for years.

- Downloading resources relating specifically to each blog post – Hubspot ($1b market cap at the time of writing).
- Automated follow up sequences for content – Infusionsoft ($500m valuation).
- Bringing the best bits of content and copywriting together – CopyBlogger (multi-million dollar businesses Synthesis and Rainmaker, among others).
- Commercial blogging – Jason Calacanis with Weblogs Inc. ($30m exit).

Being first isn't easy, but if you can do it, it can set you up for the life of your business.

It's easy to look back with 20/20 hindsight and say these guys were clearly onto something. It's much harder to be the pioneer yourself for the modern age. One framework that can point you in the right direction is provided by Peter Thiel in his book, *Zero To One*.

The book is about creating companies, but its core purpose is to provide a framework for creating something that is revolutionary by answering one simple question: "What is one thing you believe to be true that most do not?" This is taking a contrarian position.

Pat Flynn believed that he would capture more value for his business if he released his revenue figures rather than worry about the value lost by giving up his secrets.

This belief is essentially the message in this book: "Take the content marketing leap of faith."

Yes, you do lose something when you "give away the farm", as Neil Patel calls it. But you stand to gain much more if you can make it work.

If you can't answer that question, you can fall back on this quote from the book: "If you want to create and capture lasting value, don't build an undifferentiated commodity business."

In other words, it's not enough to enter into a highly competitive area (online content) and produce an undifferentiated product. You have to do something unique. So analyze your content and compare it to what else is out there. How many other people are doing content like you? If everyone is doing it, then why would people pay attention to you?

Being a pioneer is not for everyone. Even these days, I get a lot of flak for our monthly reports despite entrepreneurs like Pat paving the way before me. But if you come to a decision based on a strong belief (that you accept and others don't share), then you are equipped for dealing with the backlash.

Whether you see yourself as a pioneer or not, you should still have some fundamental beliefs driving your business and your content. That will be a good step towards differentiating yourself and standing out from the crowd.

The Opportunist

"Newsjacking" is a term coined by David Meerman Scott to describe taking someone's news story, attaching yourself to it, and riding the wave. Journalists do it all the time, sometimes releasing five or six follow up stories about the same thing with a slightly different angle, because they know the story already has people's attention.

It's a similar technique to what we do with the content multiplier framework: take something that works and do more of it. The only difference is, in this case we are taking it from someone else. Borrowing it, perhaps.

This is what an opportunist does. Figures out what already has traction and creates something, ideally in a unique way, around that topic.

Elisa Doucette, who has an online column on Forbes called **Shattering Glass** (http://www.forbes.com/sites/elisadoucette/), uses this technique often when determining what kind of topics to cover there.

In November of 2014, she was looking over the trending topics on Twitter and noticed a news story that looked interesting to her. Since she was working on a book proposal about shame and criticism, she had a lot to say about some online bullying of President Obama's daughters at the White House's annual turkey pardoning ceremony (yes, that's actually a thing in the United States).

As a result, her article[2] received over half a million views in less than 24 hours and helped to establish her as an authority in the niche, and got her appearances on outlets like Sirius News Radio and Huffington Post TV.

Within six months, she was meeting with agents and publishers in New York to discuss the book proposal that was just an idea before that post hit. As an editor that provides feedback and critiques on content every day, she made a great impact with one trending story that she was able to add a unique perspective on.

Catching one of these waves can get you a huge amount of attention, so it's worth having a look to see if you can use this strategy.

How To Be An Opportunist

This strategy can be used by any business owner, as long as they deeply understand their audience. If you know who they are and what they care about, it's not hard to work out what topics to cover.

Here are a few specific ways you can do it:

Google AdWords Keyword Planner

1. Visit the **Google AdWords Keyword Planner** (https://adwords.google.com/ko/KeywordPlanner/).
2. Enter some keywords that describe the sort of content you want to create—for example, I'll enter "Craft Beer" if I am working on Black Hops Brewing.
3. Click "Get ideas".
4. Click the "Keyword Ideas" tab to just see the individual keyword ideas.
5. Use the "Keyword Filters" on the left to only show keywords with a certain amount of searches. I generally look for keywords with between 200-500 searches for a new site, or more for an established site. In the example above I can see quite a few keywords in the 1,000-2,000 searches range, including keywords like "brewing equipment", "homebrew recipes", "best craft beers", and "craft beer festival". All of these would make a good starting point for some content.

Creating content using those keywords doesn't mean you will automatically rank well in Google for the keywords, but it does tell you that they are topics people care about.

Google Trends

Google Trends (http://google.com/trends/) is great if you already have some idea of what you are looking for. You can use it to see very quickly what the hot topics are right now.

For example, let's look at a few different beer styles with the idea that we'd write a post about how to brew a certain beer style. I know the main styles already, so let's put them into Google Trends and see what comes up.

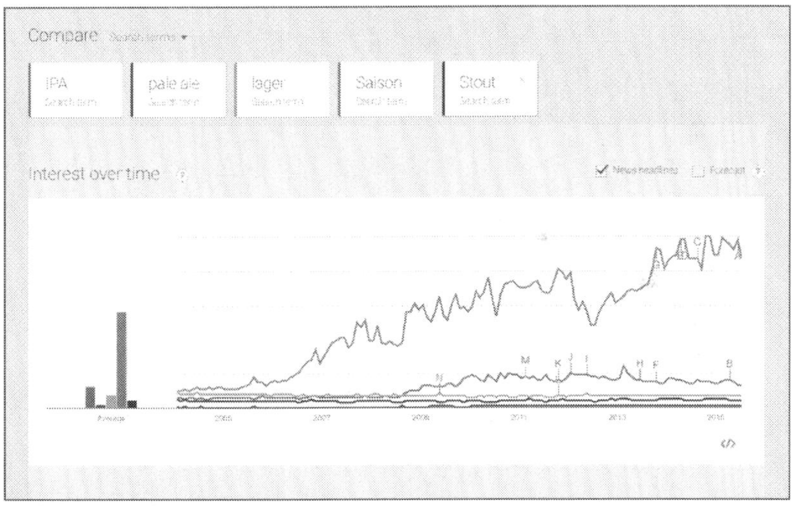

Looking at this chart, I would opt to write a post about how to brew a Saison, because it's a gradually rising trend. If you can find a trend that has a sharp, recent rise, that could be even better.

BuzzSumo

BuzzSumo (http://buzzsumo.com/) is another great tool that finds content popular in your industry right now.

All you have to do is enter the topic, and it will show you a bunch of posts that have done well in your industry.

Again using the craft beer example, here are the results.

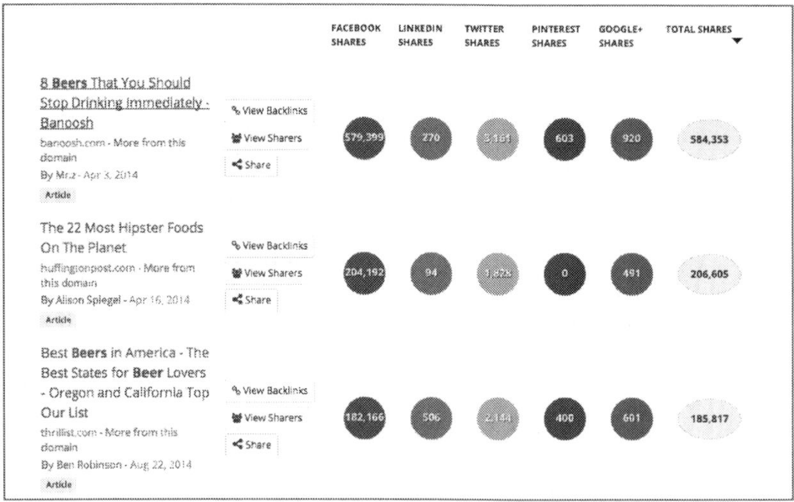

You can learn a lot from content listed here. One easy option is to apply the content ideas to your location. For example, since Black Hops Brewing is only in Australia, I could go with any of these topics:

1. 6 Australian beers you should stop drinking immediately.
2. The 12 most hipster breweries in Australia.

3. Our list of the best Australian craft beers of 2015.
4. VB sales decline, Australians now drink more craft beer than VB (if this was actually true).

Competitor Analysis

Another way to build on something that's working is through borrowing ideas from competitors. Generally, I don't choose a direct competitor but rather someone in a related industry.

So for my example, let's take the wine industry. I choose two popular wine blogs in Australia:

1. **Vinomofo** (http://vinomofo.com/content/articles)
2. **The Wine Wankers** (http://thewinewankers.com.au/)

From there, I can look for what content is either doing very well or is interesting in some way. You can do this one of two ways.

First, you can look through the blog and see if they have anything that shows you their popular posts. A lot of blogs have something in the sidebar for this. In our case, The Wine Wankers have a sidebar widget that says "The Trendy Stuff". I can use that to see a bunch of interesting articles that could apply directly to craft beer. The top one is "A great collection of wine infographics", which is a post that just embeds a bunch of infographics related to the wine industry. We could easily do the same thing for beer.

The second way you can find the top articles is to put the site into BuzzSumo. When I do that with Vinomofo, I get some interesting articles.

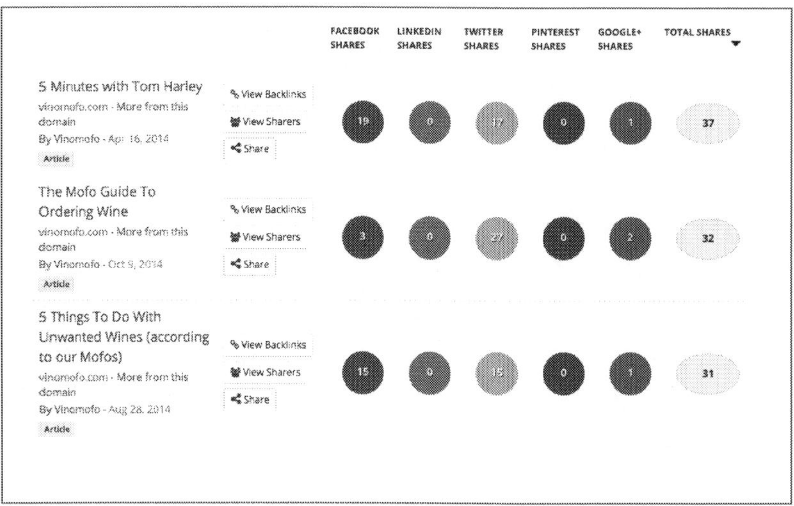

The two that stand out to me are "The Mofo Guide to Ordering Wine" and "5 Things To Do With Unwanted Wines". A guide to ordering beer would probably be quite funny since the craft beer industry is still in its infancy in Australia. The idea of your beer order being a tough decision would make a good hook for an article.

The "5 Things To Do With Unwanted Wine" article is an entertaining, BuzzFeed-style listicle. We could do something similar with beer, and it probably hasn't been done, e.g.,

"Pour it into a Budweiser bottle and give it to your non-craft, beer-drinking friends".

Resource Jacking

The final way you can go about creating content that is trendy right now is through utilizing the resources of much bigger companies. BuzzFeed is a perfect example.

At the time of writing, the company is valued at close to one billion dollars, employs 700+ people, and gets 150 million unique visitors per month.

A company like that knows a *lot* about content. They have people who live and breathe split testing headlines, they have their finger on every pulse, and they can create content that impacts people within minutes of spotting a trend.

So why not use what they have and learn from them? Examine what content is currently getting a lot of attention, and see how you can apply that to your own content. Look at what headlines they are using right now, what media they are using, etc. You can do this with direct competitors, companies you look up to, or media giants like BuzzFeed. Anyone bigger than you, with more experience and more money, leaves a good trail of what they have learned spending their money.

BuzzFeed also has a whole bunch of categories—for example, food. One look at the most popular posts in the Food category gives me a stack of content ideas for my craft beer business.

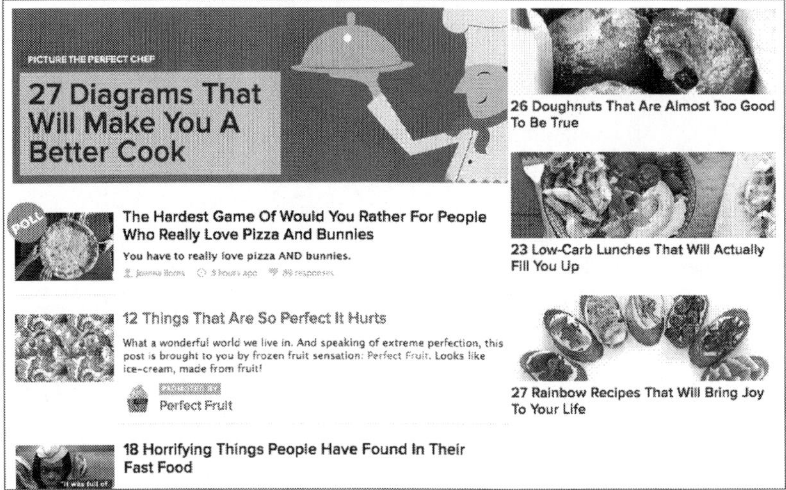

How about:

- 12 beers that are so perfect it hurts.
- 18 horrifying facts about mainstream beer consumption.
- 12 craft beers that are almost too crazy to be true (look at some wild beers like some of the ones done by the *Brew Dogs* TV show).

With these ideas alone, our blog is starting to look pretty interesting!

The Reporter

Jason Calacanis is the guy I think of when I think about journalism and startups. He got started in the early days of the web when he created a magazine about startups in New York called *Silicon Alley Reporter*.

When blogging was becoming prominent in the 90's, Jason hired the world's best content creators and built a network of news blogs called Weblogs Inc. The network included sites like Engadget and Autoblog and was eventually sold to AOL for around $30 million. He didn't stop there. In the years since, he's embraced a bunch of different projects all around the idea of reporting on the news in unique ways.

- **This Week in Startups** (http://thisweekinstartups.com/) is one of the original and most well-respected podcasts on technology news and startups. Jason hosts the show with an award-winning team, and it generates half a million dollars in advertising revenue per year. His news roundup episodes bring in journalists and startup founders to discuss the week's news in tech and startups.
- The Launch Ticker is an email which summarises startup news and contains comments from industry heavyweights.
- His app, **[Inside]** (http://inside.com), is a curated summary of news stories from around the world. You

can vote up, comment on, or share the stories, all of which impacts on what other people see in the app.

- He writes a weekly email and regular content on his site, often opinion pieces about a news item in the industry.
- He created and hosts the world's largest startup conference, **LAUNCH Festival** (http://www.launchfestival.com/), where he showcases the latest emerging startups.

Jason has always been passionate about reporting on the news and providing his own opinions. Being a startup guy means he's been able to evolve the way he executes that over time. He knows the news is always going to be interesting and is constantly looking for innovative ways to both deliver it and monetize it.

How To Be A Reporter

The first question here is: can you report on the news in your industry in a way that other people aren't doing? Perhaps the typical news is bland, boring, or nonexistent. Or perhaps you have something unique to offer, like your style or the delivery format.

As a business owner, you can report on the news in your industry in a number of different ways.

Here are a bunch of ideas:

- Podcast – Grab some other industry experts and jump on Skype to chat about what is happening in the industry. Use **Pamela for Skype** (http://www.pamela.biz/) or **Ecamm Call Recorder** (http://www.ecamm.com/mac/callrecorder/) to record the call, publish it on your blog, and submit the feed to iTunes. I have a podcasting guide linked up at http://contentmachine.com/resources that will help.
- Video – Do the same thing as Podcasts, but use **Google Hangouts** (http://www.google.com/hangouts) or **YouTube Live** (https://www.youtube.com/) and publish the video to YouTube.
- Roundup post – A roundup post is where you summarise what other people are saying in one of your own posts. It's easy to do with news. Visit the top news sites in your space and write a summary of the top stories for your own audience.
- Publish an opinion piece – If you have a strong opinion about something that is doing the rounds at the moment, write something up and publish it. **Medium** (http://medium.com) is a good platform for publishing high quality, original content like this.
- Email – Do a weekly email summarizing what's happening in your industry.
- Publish some original journalism – Probably not the easiest thing to do, but original journalism certainly can get a lot of attention if it's done well.

The Artist

You don't have to go far these days to see the impact that visuals are having on online content.

1. Images on Facebook get 54% more "Likes" than text posts.
2. Photos on Twitter have a much higher "Retweet" rate (35% according to one study, 150% according to another).
3. The image-based social networks Tumblr, Pinterest, and Instagram are the fastest-growing social platforms in the world (faster than Twitter, Facebook, and LinkedIn).

The fact is, people love images. The problem is, it's hard to come up with high-quality images if you aren't a designer yourself. For that reason, they often aren't done well, which creates a great opportunity.

Frank Body (http://frankbody.com) has done a remarkable job of using visuals to blow up a multi-million dollar business out of thin air. Well, not air, but unused recycled coffee beans.

In early 2013, a regular customer walked into a cafe in Melbourne and asked for some used coffee to be used as an exfoliate. Steve Rowley, the owner of the cafe, naturally saw this as a business opportunity. Who wouldn't?

Speaking with his partner, Bree Johnson, and her business partners, Erika Geraerts and Jess Hatzis of marketing firm **Willow and Blake** (http://willowandblake.com), they decided to research the availability of coffee scrubs online. Apart from DIY recipes, there was no business marketing such a product, particularly through visuals. They had worked in other industries using visual marketing on Instagram and achieved dramatic results.

Steve also called on the help of friend Alex Boffa. Conveniently, the group was travelling to Bali, where they were able to try coffee scrubs at the local resort spas. After further research they realized that they had to use fresh coffee grounds to maintain the caffeine content, but that some of the potential benefits of using coffee included treating skin conditions such as acne, cellulite, psoriasis, and stretch marks.

What started off as a fun trip quickly turned into a booming business. Four months of product development spent trialing different oils and complimentary exfoliates resulted in their original scrub. With the help of branding agency **For The Love And Money** (http://fortheloveandmoney.com), the team created the Frank Body Scrub and brand.

They set up an account on **Instagram** (http://instagram.com/frank_bod) and promoted the hashtag #thefrankeffect, and customers from all around the world began sharing their pictures.

This was the result of a fairly aggressive social media and PR campaign, utilizing bloggers and Instagram personalities to share their product with various networks.

At the time of writing, less than two years after launch, their account has over 600,000 followers. They have sold products to thousands of customers around the world and are likely to pass $20M in annual revenue for 2015[3].

It's a remarkable story and obviously a viral success that is never easy to replicate. However, it really demonstrates the power of visual marketing on modern social platforms. Pictures of women in the shower covered with coffee grounds is content marketing. As it turns out, extremely effective content marketing.

How To Be An Artist

Utilizing the power of images could mean adding some images to existing content, or it could mean creating brand new, image-heavy content.

Here are eleven ways you can go about ramping up your image content.

1. Screenshots

If you have any kind of software-related business, screenshots are a super easy way to add visuals to your content. **Skitch** (https://evernote.com/skitch/) and **Jing** (http://techsmith.com/jing.html) are great tools for creating screenshots.

2. Charts And Graphs

People love charts, and with tools like Google Docs, it's simple and free to come up with intelligently designed, interesting charts. We use them in our monthly report posts on our blog. I also use them regularly when I present at conferences. Flowcharts are another good way to show ideas, and **Lucidchart** (http://lucidchart.com) is a handy tool for creating them.

3. SlideShares

SlideShare (http://slideshare.net) is a site for uploading visual presentations that is definitely worth a look. SlideShare is its own platform with its own visitors, so you can reach a new audience. You can also embed SlideShares in your own site, making your blog posts that much richer. It's also a great option for repurposing content. You can pick any content you've written or spoken about before, redo it in PowerPoint, and make it into a SlideShare.

Gary Vaynerchuk has some great examples up on his account (http://www.slideshare.net/vaynerchuk/). Just remember that there's no audio, so the best SlideShares will have just the right amount of text with strong images, all to give the slide context and entice the visitor to keep clicking through.

4. Custom Illustrations

Custom illustrations can be a great way to differentiate your content from the crowd. Big budget publications like newspapers do it, but the average business isn't that far along.

You can use illustrations for featured images or elements within posts. **Help Scout** (http://www.helpscout.net/blog/) and **Groove** (https://www.groovehq.com/blog) are both great examples of this. Both stand out above the noise because they "look" completely different to everything else out there.

5. Screenshares, Webinars, And Video Courses

If you have an educational focus for your content, screenshares and videos are a great way to get the learning across. Video training platforms like **Udemy (**https://www.udemy.com**/)** and **Coursera** (https://www.coursera.org/) are exploding and the technical barrier is being wiped away.

All you need to create a decent screenshare video is a USB headset and screen capture software like **Camtasia** (http://techsmith.com/camtasia.html) or **ScreenFlow** (http://telestream.net/screenflow/overview.htm). Video is more difficult, but if you can do it well, it helps elevate your authority to a new level.

Marie Forleo (http://marieforleo.com) is a great place to get inspiration when it comes to doing online videos well.

6. Visual Social Apps

Emerging social visual platforms like **Vine** (https://vine.co/), **Periscope** (https://www.periscope.tv/) and **Instagram** (https://instagram.com/) have created a huge opportunity for people willing to create great content that engages people.

On these platforms, there are plenty of examples like Frank Body who have built a huge community and leveraged that community to create a great business. Video is also exploding in popularity on other social networks like Facebook and Twitter.

For some people, it might not be the right platform. But if it's a good fit then it can be extremely beneficial.

7. Infographics

Infographics give you a few benefits over traditional content. For starters, not many people are doing them well. So if *you* can, then you will stand out. You can also post them on image-specific platforms like Pinterest and get your message out to new audiences. Furthermore, you'll have created an embeddable resource which other people can either link back to or embed directly, thereby getting more eyeballs on your content and generating backlinks.

There are three main ways to create an infographic:

1. Use an infographic builder like **Visme** (http://visme.co/) or **Piktochart** (http://piktochart.com/).
2. If you have reasonable image editing skills, you can buy Infographic elements from sites like **ThemeForest** (http://themeforest.net) and customize them yourself to create your own infographic.
3. You can pay a designer to build a custom infographic. You can find affordable designers on **99Designs** (http://99Designs.com) and high quality designers on **Crew** (https://crew.co/).

8. Quotable Social Images

Another easy way to add images to your content is to create quotable social media images. **Canva** (http://canva.com) is a great free tool that lets you create them with very little graphical expertise. These can be used to improve existing content or simply work as stand alone images on social networks like Facebook, Pinterest, or Instagram. You can even build great-looking social media quotes directly on your phone using apps like **WordSwag** (http://wordswag.co).

Here are a few simple ways to do it:

- Create a personal image. Use an image of yourself and one of your own quotes.
- Quote a guest or author. This is useful if you have had someone on a podcast or mentioned them in a blog post.
- Ask a question. What would someone ask that your content can answer? Use an image to ask the question and prime the visitor for the problem you solve or for starting a conversation.
- Show a stat. If you have simple statistics that you want to stand out in your article, place them in an interesting image.
- If you want to post general quotes, put the word into Pinterest and see what images come up. Some people re-post other people's images, while many more re-brand the quotes while making sure to mention the original creator.

9. Memes

Memes are a little different than a quotable social image and have potential for viral sharing. Memes are usually funny, ironic, and leverage pop culture.

BuzzFeed articles typically feature lots of these, and they tend to be funny and quick to skim through and get the gist of.

Meme Generator (http://memegenerator.net) is one of many sites and apps you can use to take popular memes and add your own text. Be sure this imagery is appropriate for your audience.

Remember to make sure you fully understand the meme and use it in the right context. People will be very quick to jump all over someone using a meme in the wrong context, and you will look out of touch.

10. Animated GIFs

Animated GIFs and autoplay videos stand out as a big trend at the moment. GIFs are being used regularly on websites now for things like showing you how to use software.

GifGrabber (http://www.gifgrabber.com/) is a simple tool for putting together animated GIFs for software usage.

BuzzFeed (http://buzzfeed.com) uses funny animated GIFs on a lot of their posts. Social networks like Instagram and Facebook are now autoplaying videos without sound. Even if you don't like it, I'm willing to bet you watch more videos on Facebook than you used to!

A really simple way we've used these in our content is by animating the charts in our monthly reports. It adds a bit of interest to the report, and we can convert that to a video file for Facebook so people can see our growth chart going up directly on the page.

11. Interactive Visuals

Adding interactive elements goes a long way towards capturing the attention of your audience. They will likely get hooked on the functionality of the interaction and stick around to consume the content.

A great example of an interactive piece of content is Matthew Daniels' Rapper Vocab chart.[4] It counts the number of individual words used by the major hip hop artists and plots them on a chart. You can mouse over the artist to see their name, so it also has a neat interactive element. This got the world's attention in 2014 and so far has amassed just under half a million likes, comments, and shares on Facebook.[5] [6] [7]

How Are You Going To Differentiate?

I hope this chapter has given you a few ideas about how you might stand out from the competition. Perhaps you are going to run with one of these strategies; maybe you will combine a few of them; or maybe you'll come up with something yourself. You might want to try a bunch of them and see what gets traction.

Whatever you do, don't ignore the differentiation piece. It could be the difference between creating content with no traction for years versus blowing up an audience overnight.

It's Now Time To Build The Machine

You now understand the fundamentals and you are ready to go with content ideas, a strategy, and a point of difference.

You are ready to build the content machine and create a scalable system for creating, managing, and growing your content marketing efforts for the purpose of growing your business.

In the next chapter we will build your content machine.

Notes

1. Pat Flynn, "SPI 071: Successful Start Ups, Millions Lost and Everything In-Between: Inside the Mind of Noah Kagan from AppSumo," *The Smart Passive Income Blog* (blog), June 19, 2013, http://www.smartpassiveincome.com/spi-071-successful-start-ups-millions-lost-and-everything-in-between-inside-the-mind-of-noah-kagan-from-appsumo/.
2. Ibid, "The Art Of Online Apologies And Why Elizabeth Lauten Failed Miserably At Hers," Shattering Glass, Forbes online, last modified December 1, 2014, http://www.forbes.com/sites/elisadoucette/2014/11/30/the-art-of-apologies-and-why-elizabeth-lauten-failed-miserably-at-hers/.
3. Mat Beeche, "After only 18 months in business Frank Body will likely exceed $20 million in revenue this year," Startup Daily, last modified February 25, 2015, http://www.startupdaily.net/2015/02/18-months-business-frank-body-will-likely-exceed-20-million-revenue-year/.
4. Matthew Daniels, "The Largest Vocabulary in Hip Hop," last modified June 2014, http://rappers.mdaniels.com.s3-website-us-east-1.amazonaws.com/.
5. Simon Rogers, "What fuels a Tweet's engagement?" Twitter Blog (blog), Twitter, Inc., last modified March 10, 2014, https://blog.twitter.com/2014/what-fuels-a-tweets-engagement.

6. Belle Beth Cooper, "How Twitter's Expanded Images Increase Clicks, Retweets and Favorites [New Data]," Buffer Social (blog), Buffer, last modified November 13, 2013, https://blog.bufferapp.com/the-power-of-twitters-new-expanded-images-and-how-to-make-the-most-of-it.
7. Ingrid Lunden, "Tumblr Overtakes Instagram As Fastest-Growing Social Platform, Snapchat Is The Fastest-Growing App," TechCrunch, AOL Inc., last modified November 25. 2014, http://techcrunch.com/2014/11/25/tumblr-overtakes-instagram-as-fastest-growing-social-platform-snapchat-is-the-fastest-growing-app/.

CHAPTER 5

SCALE: BUILDING THE MACHINE

You've come a long way! Understanding the fundamentals puts you miles ahead of the competition right from the start. Focusing on creating high-quality content establishes you as an expert worth following. Finding a differentiator will help you get noticed.

The final piece is figuring out a way to build a business off the back of this content, then growing and sustaining the strategy in the long term. I call this "Building The Machine."

Design And Conversion

If you are going to run with content marketing as an important strategy in your business, then design and conversion are critical components. Design will impact everything you do, and if you have bad design, you will never know. It will never show up in Analytics. People will never tell you. They will just dismiss you as not being legitimate or serious.

If you have an established business, please don't underestimate the importance of design. Employ a designer or pay a high-quality design firm to make sure whatever content you do is well designed.

If you are just getting started, stick to my seven rules for hacking design early on:

1. Use a nice theme and don't touch it.
2. Remove anything not completely necessary.
3. Make alignment and padding symmetrical.
4. Look down to the single pixel level (every last detail counts; one pixel out could mean visitors not "feeling right" about your site).
5. Benchmark off the best, but don't ever copy.
6. Don't have a logo unless you can afford a good one.
7. You aren't a designer, and neither are your friends on Facebook. Get design advice from design experts.

Your site should also be set up for conversion. This is a concept closely tied to design. A well-designed site will mean a site that looks good, will work for its intended audience, and converts well.

Most people see conversions as something that can be easily measured. I don't. You can measure how many people opt in to your aggressive pop-up, but you can't measure how many people won't trust you, because you are taking before you are giving.

If you focus on quality, your well-designed brand, and trust, you will convert visitors into customers over time. If you try to do it prematurely (with excessively aggressive tactics like overzealous pop-ups and exit scripts), then your conversions on Analytics might go up, but your long-term brand will be damaged.

There are three different ways to create these conversion funnels which I'll address now.

Defining Your Funnel

I've mentioned a few times that I want you to think of yourself as a content marketer and not a blogger. That's how important it is. Marketers need a funnel. A funnel is a way to transition the broad members of the community down to a smaller group of customers. Put another way, how does someone go from a blog reader to a customer of your product or service? This is where the monetization logic is put into practice.

The way you design your funnel will impact every aspect of your content.

There's no "one size fits all", but I've found three popular options that work well.

1. The email funnel
2. The product funnel
3. The content funnel

The Email Funnel

Neil Patel of **Quick Sprout** (http://quicksprout.com) creates great content. But he's a busy guy, and it's just him, so he's lucky to do two or three posts a week. Instead, he goes in hard for the email opt in.

He's got huge pop-ups that cover the whole site and force you to click "No, I don't want more traffic" to close them. He's got sidebar opt ins, mid-post opt ins, and an exit script that will create an opt in pop-up form when you try to leave the page.

Typically when sites are direct with email opt in, they are also quite direct with the emails themselves. Once you sign up, you get regular emails (sometimes daily or even more often) that try to deliver you more good content but also try to frame you up for purchasing.

This is one way of funnelling visitors down, and it works well for Neil.

If you want to look at this strategy, **SumoMe** (http://sumome.com), **OptimizePress** (http://www.optimizepress.com), and **LeadPages** (http://leadpages.net) are the two leading tools for building email opt ins.

The Product Funnel

The product funnel is where the main call to action on the site is using your product. Email opt ins are nowhere to be seen. If you like the content, your only option is to visit the landing page and sign up for the service.

This tends to be the default position people take. When they start a blog they'll fill the sidebar with product information, and they'll keep the standard business menu across the top. This is generally a mistake, because content marketing is about creating value for others. It's hard to do that when you are so focused on yourself.

However, there are ways to execute this well. It works very efficiently with free software and tools, because people love signing up for those, and you are also building an email list when they sign up.

Buffer (https://blog.bufferapp.com/) is well-versed in this method. They have a big banner across the top to sign in with Facebook or Twitter. The site has a scroll opt in down at the bottom that asks you to "Schedule your first post". They also give away documents and resources completely free with no email opt in. Just with a simple note at the bottom says, "Save time on social media with Buffer. Schedule your first post now!"

They also do a great job with the content itself. By using the product funnel, you can intertwine your product with your content. You can get customers to help you with content, release case studies, do product demonstrations, and much more. As long as this content is "good content", then it can be a smart way to regularly mention your product without coming across as a salesperson. Buffer has a big content team that does all of this and more on a daily basis.

As a service, Buffer has a very broad audience: virtually anyone with a business who uses social media. That means almost everyone reading their blog is a potential customer. So this product funnel works quite well.

Once you've signed up for the app, there is also a sophisticated email sequence that occurs, but it's nothing like what you'd get from a more direct email funnel.

Since this structure generally works when you have a significantly broad product and low-friction signups (like a free software service), it's not the best option for most people.

The Content Funnel

The content funnel is my personal preference. It aims to build an email list, but it also favours content and brand over email opt ins. It requires you to create a lot of content, but that shouldn't be a problem after powering through chapter three.

The content funnel works as follows:

1. You create a lot of great content and give the vast majority away on your site publicly.
2. You create a few bigger pieces of content, some of which you give away on your site publicly and some of which you put behind an email opt in.
3. When someone signs up for the emails, you have a sequence that sends them more valuable content and segments them to make sure the suitable ones are pitched on your business. It's not a heavy pitch; it's just enough to make sure you've done your job in ensuring that your most engaged audience understands what you do.

This is what we do at WP Curve. We put most of our content out in blog posts freely available on our site. Sometimes we'll support those blog posts with Google Docs, frameworks, ebooks, and downloads that keen readers can grab. We also occasionally ask for their email through a landing page or opt in at the end of a blog post.

With larger projects where trust is a must, we'll just give it all away publicly with no email opt in. That is what I do with my books. All of the frameworks, downloads, and resources for this book are freely available at http://contentmachine.com/resources. This builds trust, and people are more likely to get behind the project and share it.

Relevant Lead Magnets

One of the easiest and least intrusive ways to get people onto your email list is using post-specific lead magnets. Conversions are all about relevancy. Having a blog post about website speed followed by an opt in for "Download my weight loss ebook" will not convert well, regardless of how well-designed it is or how aggressive you are with the opt in. However, if you put an opt in for a downloadable 14-point website speed check at the end of the post, it will convert very well.

You can do the same thing with scroll opt ins, landing pages, pop-ups, sidebar opt ins, or any other kind of opt in form. The key point is making the lead magnet relevant to the post.

Of course, it takes a bit of effort to add a different opt in to every post—not to mention setting up the website and email sequences to support providing the lead magnet. I think the best way to do this is by checking your top posts and making sure all of them have post-specific lead magnets.

If you don't have many posts just yet, you can go on gut feeling and add them to the posts you think will be winners. If you've built up a good library of content, I'd suggest automating this with **Zapier** (https://zapier.com):

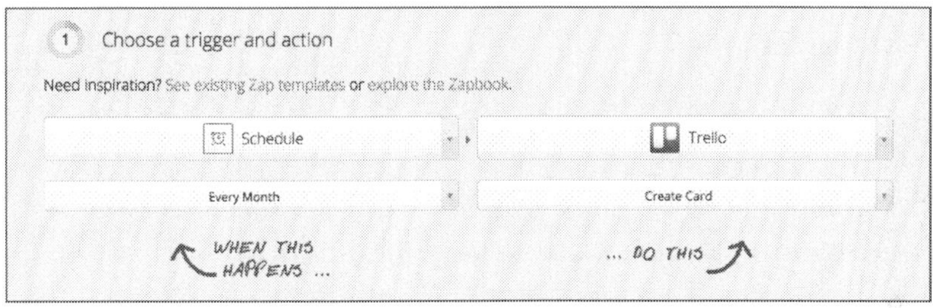

The basic idea here is to use the "Schedule" zap to automatically create a task for your admin team. I have a team of Virtual Assistants in the Philippines who look after these things for me. I use Trello to manage our tasks, but Zapier integrates with lots of different tools if you aren't a Trello user.

This is how the "Zap" works: every month the admin team is reminded to look in Google Analytics under Behaviour/Site content at a year's worth of data to see the top 25 posts. They manually check through each post to see if there is a post-specific opt in at the end. If they don't find one, they will contact our content marketing manager and recommend that we put one together.

To collect email addresses you can use an email marketing tool like **MailChimp** (http://mailchimp.com) or **Infusionsoft** (http://infusionsoft.com) (I use both), and an accompanying plugin like **OptinSkin** (http://optinskin.com) or **LeadPages** (http://leadpages.net).

Five Must-Have Sequences For Content Marketers

Once you have email addresses, you need to do something with them. Here are five sequences that I've used to get the full benefit out of obtaining an email address.

1. Content Drip Or Weekly Email

If people have opted in to hear more from you, you first need to make sure they will actually hear more from you. I like the idea of doing a weekly email, because the content is always fresh and people feel much more part of the community when they are engaging in up-to-date content.

Sending a weekly email can be consistently time consuming. So if you don't have time, or you prefer, set up a content drip sequence.

A content drip sequence is a series of pre-written emails that will send out useful content to the person on a set schedule. I try to be as generous as possible with the content without being blatantly sales-y. The goal is to build trust and build up desire for your product/service at the same time. You can do this via an automation in MailChimp, or a sequence in a program like Infusionsoft. When the time is right in this sequence, you may want to pitch your product or service.

Another good method to drip content is to offer an email training course as the opt in lead magnet on your site. This sets up the visitor with the expectation that you will be emailing them information over the coming days or weeks.

2. Content Suggestion Sequence

I like to have one simple email that gets sent to subscribers asking them what they would like to hear about. If you are using content in your business and you want it to get traction, you need to learn what people want. So what better way than to ask them? When someone subscribes to your list for the first time, have your system send them a simple email that just asks them what topics they are interested in hearing more about.

If you let people reply to your emails, then you actually read and reply back, you will build a legion of close fans. Often people will ask for something that you've already covered, but they didn't know. That's a great opportunity to be helpful, point them to it, and build that trust further. If they suggested something you hadn't thought of, then add it to your ideas list.

3. Pitch Sequence

At various stages in your campaigns, you might find a good time to pitch someone on your service. But what if the person has subscribed to four or five of your campaigns, and they are heavily engaged with your message already? It wouldn't be productive to constantly pitch to them.

To ensure I'm not pitching the same people over and over again, I like to have a pitch sequence. I use Infusionsoft, which makes this sort of thing pretty easy. At one stage during a campaign I will tag the visitor to be pitched. This is automated inside Infusionsoft.

They will then enter the pitch sequence, and the first step of that sequence is to remove them if they've been pitched recently. That timeframe will depend on your business—it could be weeks or months. If they aren't removed, they are pitched on your service and tagged so they will be removed next time if they enter the sequence again. I also exclude current customers—you don't want to be preaching to the converted.

You can get as sophisticated as you like with this. With more advanced CRMs like Infusionsoft, you can "lead score" and only pitch people when they hit a certain level. For most small businesses, just a simple pitch sequence is a good place to start.

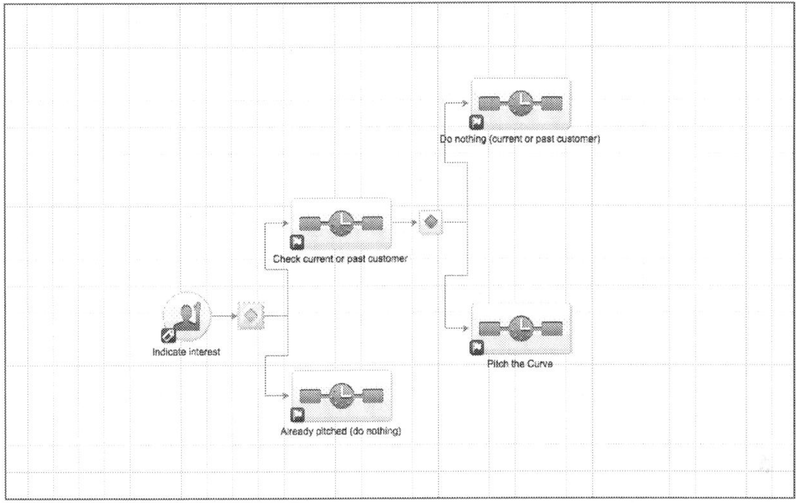

4. Cart Abandonment

One very easy sequence you can add to any business is a cart abandonment sequence. This is a bit outside of the content marketing topic, but because it's such a simple high-impact task to perform (and many people don't remember to do it), I thought I'd mention it.

Through this sequence, you email people who went some way towards purchasing but didn't finalize the transaction. This could mean the actual shopping cart software has steps, and the customer completed step one but did not make it to step four. Regardless, your process for signing up customers should involve a form where the first field is an email address. If people fill in the email address but not the rest, then they are ripe for a cart abandonment email.

You can send this even if they don't save the form if you set it to save the email dynamically as they fill it out. Once their email is entered they are tagged for the sequence, and if they don't complete the purchase, they receive an email notification.

The email is very simple—it just says something like what I've put below. If your product or service is image-central, then include some nice images to entice the person back.

> *We noticed you visited [site] but didn't complete your order.*
>
> *We don't want you to miss out, so if you want to finalize your purchase, please click here to return to the site.*
>
> *If you are having any issues with the checkout, please reply and we will help you out.*
>
> *Looking forward to working with you.*
>
> *[company name]*

5. Problem Based Conversion Sequence

When someone buys from you it's generally because your product or service solves a problem for them. However, it may not be the same problem for everyone, so it's a good idea to dig into what these problems are and exactly how you solve them. Once you understand that, you can then have sequences that pitch your product or service around solving these specific issues.

For example, with WP Curve, we solve hundreds of WordPress problems. But for most people, they will sign up for one of six reasons:

1. Their site is slow, and they want us to make it faster.
2. Their site is not secure, and they don't want to be hacked.
3. They want someone to maintain their site proactively, so they don't have to worry about the technical issues.
4. They want to rank better in Google, so they want the simple SEO factors under control.
5. They want to convert more visitors to email subscribers or customers.
6. They want more traffic for their site / blog.

These problems become your major topic areas. For each one you put together:

1. A banner ad you can use to market your services to these people based specifically around that topic, i.e., "A faster site means higher Google rankings. Join WP Curve to speed up your site for as little as $79".
2. An email sequence you can use to email people who are interested in this line of content. Use a simple

sequence that sends them some interesting info and has a specific call to action based around that topic.
3. A lot of content on your site that discusses that exact topic.

You then do two things on any of the posts on your site that discuss those topics:

1. You use a service like **AdRoll** (http://Adroll.com) or native Facebook Retargeting to add a specific tracking pixel to that piece of content. When they visit other sites around the web, they will see that specific ad, as opposed to a generic ad for your service.
2. Put together a category-based lead magnet, so any time you create content around that topic, you have a call to action that gets people to opt in. They are then put on the sequence in step 2 above.

You can either do this manually or using a plugin for putting certain lead magnets on every post within a certain category on your site.

To ensure you aren't *constantly* pitching to potential customers, I would also put some limits on it. For example, create a monthly limit that no one is pitched more than once during that month.

Manage Influencers

I would not have been noticed at all if I hadn't worked from day one on engaging influencers. It's extremely hard to get noticed. Even if my content was great, I still needed to get it in front of the right people.

In chapter three, we identified influencers as part of the content strategy. But what about long term? How do you build up a relationship with them and maintain that to keep it strong? This needs to be built into your ongoing processes or into your values as a person.

For me, it wasn't a structured process so much as just a general approach which said, "Any time I can help out an influencer or give them special attention, I will." Of course, any time I *can* help out anyone I generally try to. That is, perhaps, the better way to think about it. But I'm only human and I won't lie: when I see an opportunity to help an influencer, I do give them special attention.

It started out with mentioning people in my blog posts and linking to their sites. I would then ask them to be on my podcast, which they generally would, and that would be a great way to break the ice and get to know them.

I'd comment on their blogs and stick up for them online. I'd look for any way to help, and I'd support whatever they were working on at the time.

Over time I was noticed and gradually started seeing benefits. I was mentioned in podcasts or on other blogs. I was invited onto other podcasts to be interviewed or invited to conferences to present. Big name influencers shared my content, and I then had a bit more leeway to email them and ask them for a hand.

This was also aided by the fact that I was creating high-quality, differentiated content that they were comfortable putting their name behind. If I was just churning out short, low-quality posts on broad topics, they may have known who I was, but they wouldn't be comfortable helping me or promoting my work.

In some cases I really went out of my way to build a relationship with an influencer, like offering to build their website for free or flying interstate to have lunch with them.

These things do take time, but I eventually got to a point where I had a big list of people who I would happily email and could directly ask for their help. I will email all of them when I launch this book, in fact, and specifically ask them to share it. Some will, some won't, but most will read my email and consider it. This has turned into some very tangible partnerships for my business and a huge boost for my content.

I'd love to reveal a list of steps for this, but I don't think that's really how influencer outreach works. You just give,

give, give, and then when you think you've given too much, you give a bit more. Sometimes when you feel like it's all for nothing, they will surprise you with something big. That's happened to me more than once.

If it suits you better, you can take a more structured approach, where you or your team have certain tasks to perform regularly for your influencers.

Here are a few ideas to run with:

- Comment on their blog, and be positive. Constant negativity will kill your reputation. The occasional challenge is fine, but watch out for unproductive criticism.
- Include them on your own blog when you do expert roundups, or link to them as examples. When you promote the post, be sure to let them know (this is part of the content promotion process we will run through later). I like to link back to their specific posts rather than their homepage. If they use WordPress and they have the trackbacks setting on, it will email them and tell them that you have linked to them.
- Follow them on social media. Consider coming to their aid if haters do their thing. Be active in sharing their posts.

- Give them free services or products from your business. If it's relevant, then everyone appreciates this.
- Invite them on a podcast to help spread their message. Ask them if there's anything else you can help with.
- Offer to help them with something that's in your area of expertise. I've had people offer to help me for free on projects who then became staff members and business partners.
- Make an effort to visit them if they are in town. I've flown interstate specifically to meet people before—it's well worth it in the end.
- Email your list with some useful content or info on their service. Let them know to expect a bit of extra traffic.
- If they have a podcast, leave an iTunes review. If they have a book, leave an Amazon review. I wouldn't hesitate emailing them to thank them and point them to the review.
- If they ever publicly ask for help for anything like a survey or a social share, jump on it.
- If they have services or products that you could benefit from, then sign up and become a customer.
- If they have an online community (free or paid), sign up and be a good community member who adds constant value and asks for nothing.

Over time you can test the waters with some sort of more formalized partnership. For example, perhaps you can create an ebook together or promote each other to your respective audiences.

These guys are busy, and it takes a lot to get their attention. Make sure you are looking at it from their point of view, and don't be annoying.

Here are a few tools you might want to use to help with this step:

- **Inkybee** (http://www.inkybee.com/) is a tool for reaching out to other influence content creators in your niche.
- **Klout** (https://klout.com) displays a 0-100 influencer rating in Twitter next to people who engage with you. If you see someone with a high score (65+), you might want to pay them extra attention.
- **Mention** (http://mention.net) will tell you any time you are mentioned on the web. If an influencer mentions you, you might want to thank them and give them extra attention.
- **Little Bird** (http://getlittlebird.com) can provide you with lists of influencers in your niche.
- **Followerwonk** (http://followerwonk.com) is another tool for providing lists of influencers on social media.

Build An Ambassador List

When I finished *The 7 Day Startup*, I chatted with **Tom Morkes** (http://tommorkes.com), who would ultimately help me with marketing the book. The first thing he told me to do was create an ambassador list.

I knew I had a bit of a community with my content, but finding people to actually advocate on my behalf? That seemed like a bit of a stretch.

I thought to myself, "I'm not sure I'm a big enough influencer for people to want to sign up and be an ambassador." I was wrong. It turned out there was a hidden contingent of people in my audience that were more than just community members. They were people who legitimately wanted to help my project succeed.

I emailed my list and asked them to join the ambassador list, and I had 500 people click the link to join within a few days.

Tom then said, "The first thing we need to do is create a Facebook group, so we can fire up the ambassadors." Again I thought the conversion of list subscriber to Facebook would be tiny, but I took his advice. I emailed them with a request to join the Facebook group. I also updated the ambassador sequence, so future people would be emailed automatically requesting they join, and after they said yes, they'd be then asked to join us on Facebook. Around 350 of the ambassadors joined the Facebook group in the next few days. I was blown away.

When it came time to launch the book, we called on the ambassadors for help. They jumped to action, sending out tweets about the book, writing reviews on Amazon, and telling their friends to grab a copy.

After the first week the sales page had over 350 tweets, and within two weeks there were over 100 five-star reviews on Amazon.com (and more in other countries). It was an amazing response and took me by complete surprise. In the months since, the group has grown to *thousands* of people, and they jump to my aid any time I need them. Of course, it's not a one-way street—I help them out in return.

For *Content Machine*, I started a new ambassador group much earlier (six months before the release date), and at the time of writing already has over 1,000 members. (If you want to join the new group, you can type 'Content Machine' into Facebook or visit http://contentmachine.com/resources for the link.)

After this experience, I realized I probably should have been doing this all along for my content. There are some people who want to be passive consumers, but there are a lot of people who want to do more.

I'd never considered creating a formal "ambassador" list or a Facebook group just for my content, but why not? It's a win-win. The members of the group are super fans, so they are eager to help. A lot of them are at a stage in their business where I can help them, so I regularly go in and offer to review people's sites or answer questions. It's very low friction to join and doesn't cost you anything other than some time.

Here's how to do it:

When someone signs up for emails on your site, send them an email that explains your ambassador list. Here's some copy you can use as a starting point:

> *Hey [name],*
>
> *I'm excited you joined my email list. I'm a passionate entrepreneur like you, and I love to help others and share what I know.*
>
> *I wanted to let you know about a special group of people in my audience called the Ambassadors. My ambassadors help me when I need the power of a group—for example, with sharing an upcoming book or project. In return, I give them special attention and often help them out for free with their business.*
>
> *If this sounds like something that would benefit you, simply click this link, and you will be immediately*

added to the list. I will send you another email with more info if you sign up.

I hope you join me!

If you have any questions, please just reply to this email. I read and respond to any I receive.

Thanks,
[Your name/signature]

If you use a tool like Infusionsoft, you can tag people who click on the link. If you use a simpler tool, you might need to get your developer to add them to a new list or just direct them to a different opt in form. Or, even simpler, you can bypass the email list and just start the social media group. That is what I did for *Content Machine*, because I got so much traction on Facebook.

If you go with the email list, after they join, send them this:

Hey [name],

Woo hoo, I'm pumped you decided to join the Ambassador list! If you need my help with anything, please just ask.

When I need a hand from you, I will send an email, and I hope you'll jump in to help out. We've also put together a Facebook group, so we can all hang out and assist each other with smaller tasks.

Click this link to join the Facebook group.

If you aren't on Facebook, that's cool—we can just stick with email.

If you have any questions, let me know!

Talk to you soon,
[Your name/signature]

Facebook groups are *significantly* more powerful than I thought. Emails tend to be pretty formal, so I don't want to stretch the friendship and email people constantly. But our Facebook group is packed with conversations all day, every day. There's a huge active support base right there ready to help, and whenever I have free time I hop on Facebook and dive in.

I highly recommend you do this as soon as you start with content marketing. Over time you will build a loyal fan base, and you'll have a huge advantage over your competitors when it comes to sharing and promoting content.

Content Creation Style Guide

It's essential that you have a process for creating high-quality content. This could be one that you work through yourself, one that your team follows, or one that you send to external content writers.

This has been a huge asset to us. When we first started accepting guest posts, it was a total mess. Everyone was at a different level, and it ended up being more work for us to get a guest author's post right than it was for us to do our own.

The style guide became our number one asset in successfully implementing a process where around half of our content is now written by external writers, and the quality is just as high.

Here is an example of one you can use. I've also provided this at http://contentmachine.com/resources if you want a downloadable Google Doc to use yourself.

Our Audience

Put in a description here about your blog, your audience, and what they like to see. It could include something like:

"Our blog is focused on online marketing and growth. Readers are generally business owners looking to improve their sales or lead generation. We pride ourselves on content that is practical, backed with details (charts, screenshots and other companies doing X), and uses simple, conversational language."

Checklist For Content Value

This checklist should mirror the high-quality content standards you created earlier in this book. It could include the following parameters:

- Useful? Does it have utility? Tip: Write to solve an issue or pain point for a single, specific person.
- New idea? Is it a new spin on an old idea or a brand new idea altogether?
- Valuable? Will a reader get value from it?
- Actionable? Are there action steps a reader can take?
- Shareable? Is there an incentive for readers to share it?
- Eye-catching? Does the headline make you want to read it?
- Flow? Does the content flow and read well?
- Entertaining? A few chuckles are a bonus.
- Long and detailed? Developed content generally goes best with our audience.

Format

We require people to send drafts as Google Docs before putting them on the site. Google Docs makes it really easy to have multiple people working on a post at once.

Text Style Guide

This is where we put general conventions used on our site. Examples could include:

- Numerals (1) instead of numbers (one).
- Sentence case title headings (only capitalize the first letter in the first word).
- Use H2 subheadings (not bold).
- A minimum of three images per post.
- Single spaces after full stops.
- Links always open in a new tab.
- Related article links have "Related" in bold with a colon, followed by a link to the article, e.g.: **Related:** 12 ways to increase engagement through visual content.

In relation to the conventions for numbers and sentence case, we use numerals in all our posts. Similarly, using capitals for all words in a heading is more accepted. I've used those conventions in this book, but generally with content I like to be less formal and use the ones above. This is personal preference, and you can use whatever conventions you prefer.

Image Style Guide

Here is an example of requirements you might have in the images section:

No Stock Photos

We like to avoid stock images whenever possible.

Proper Image File Types

Use this to determine which file type is appropriate for the images in your post.

- **JPEG** – Good for photos of people or places or things, bad for screenshots of apps and websites or text.
- **PNG** – Good for screenshots of apps and websites with gradients. But can be problematic for file sizes.
- **GIF** – Good for flat images with no gradients. Watch out for small images inside a screenshot like a chat avatar or a gradient like the top bar of a browser.

Full Width Images

Here is an example of requirements for image file sizes. These will depend on the theme you use on your site and other factors.

All images must meet these exact requirements. If you aren't confident about optimizing and uploading the images, please send them through to us, and we can do it for you.

- All wide images to be exactly 640px wide, which means they will be full width on the site. Ideally they will be exactly 300px high, but if that doesn't work you can make them higher in increments of 100px.

- If the image doesn't suit full width, then make it 250px wide, and we will right align it. Ideally make it exactly 250px by 250px, but if it's more of a portrait and doesn't work as an exact square, then you can set the height to 350px or 450px.
- Try to keep all full width images under 70kb, but make sure they aren't blurry or pixelated.
- Try to keep all 250px images under 40kb, but make sure they aren't blurry or pixelated.
- Use .JPG for photos and medium-res PNGs or GIFs for flat vector images.
- Images should have either no border (in which case we will apply one automatically), or if they have a white background they can have a non-rounded 1px border with color #CCCCCC.
- Don't hyperlink images in WordPress, and no left/right alignment or resizing.

Featured Image

If you use featured images in WordPress, add the requirements here. Examples could include:

Each post has a featured image.

- Make the featured image exactly 120 x 120px.
- If it's a white background image, add a 1px border with color #CCCCCC.

Excerpt

Ideally, your blog homepage will show a custom excerpt of the post. Allowing WordPress to automatically use the first few sentences from the post can be a mistake. Your first few sentences might fit well in the context of the full piece, but they may not provide the best summary to entice readers to click a shared link. Instead, use the WordPress excerpts area and create a few sentences that really excite the user to click through to read the post. Here is an example guideline for excerpts.

The excerpt should be two sentences separated with a full paragraph space. The sentences should be long enough to take up two lines each. The excerpt should introduce the reader to the blog post and entice them to read on.

$66,596 monthly run rate, 11% increase in traffic, and big events – May 2015 monthly report

June 2, 2015 · 3 Comments

Revenue remains about the same, but we have made some great progress for our content and traffic.

Dan has been actively getting out to events and speaking about the WP Curve journey, he spoke at 2 great events in May.

Editing Notes

Here we generate practical editing notes and list other things to look out for. Examples could include:

When reviewing after first draft, keep an eye out for:

- *Filler words like: I think, etc, things, stuff.*
- *Long sentences with no punctuation.*
- *Long paragraphs that aren't broken up.*
- *Waffling or off-topic sentences.*
- *Double check links.*
- *Make sure links work.*
- *Make sure they open in a new tab.*

Inside WordPress

These tasks have to be performed by guest writers once the post is ready to be published. We generally give them a separate template to fill in which asks these questions. I've provided a document template up at http://contentmachine.com/resources that you can use. Here is what we include:

Put this information in a separate document with your final article.

1. SEO Meta description (less than 156 chars).
2. Focus Keyword.
3. Post Tags.
4. A link to a dropbox folder with your images.
   a. Please save your blog post images in this folder in the dimensions listed below.
   b. Include a featured image.

   c. Include a large photo of yourself to use for social sharing (we'll put a quote from the post on the photo).
5. *Title of each image.*
   a. *Name the image with keywords spaced with underscores (Monthy_Income_Chart).*
6. *A brief, two-sentence excerpt to entice readers.*
7. *One or two tweetable quotes from your post.*
8. *An author bio if this is your first submission.*

We will talk more about using these guidelines with guest writers later in this chapter.

Create A Monthly Feedback Loop

As a creative person, you might struggle with the balance between what people want to consume and what you want to create. If you are in content marketing for the purpose of building a business, then you need to follow what is doing well. As I've mentioned throughout this book, the number one reason content marketing doesn't work is that the content is simply not good enough. When you follow what works, you get closer to something that is "good enough" for your audience.

A really easy way to manage this is by doing a simply monthly check up. I schedule it in Zapier and have my content marketing manager fill in the report.

Here are a bunch of things to include in the monthly report. You can also download a Google Doc template for this up at http://contentmachine.com/resources.

10 Pieces Of Content Created

I like to set a goal each month to create a certain amount of content. I wasn't too worried about this when I was doing content for myself, but it's a good metric to have in place when you hire a content manager. Ten pieces of high-quality content per month is a reasonable output for a full-time content manager.

This assumes they are highly-researched, detailed, long, and high-impact posts. It should also give them a bit of time to work on more strategic things like managing lead magnets and email sequences.

In our business, we have the content manager do six posts and oversee four posts by external creators.

On Track For Traffic Goal (5% Growth)

Traffic should grow over time if your content is high quality. Google will start ranking the site, people will start linking to it, and influencers will start sharing it. Five percent monthly growth is aggressive but achievable, particularly early on.

On Track For Email List Goal (5% Growth)

If you are using the content funnel you want to build an email list—but not in a super aggressive way. If your traffic is growing by 5%, you should reasonably expect to grow your email list by 5% as well. This goal forces you to focus on working on lead magnets and email as well as doing new content.

One Breakout Sharing Hit (50+ Tweets)

We like to see at least one post become a breakout success during the month. We've defined a breakout hit as 50+ tweets. This is 50 real people sharing it. No auto-follower nonsense here. But look at your own results and determine what represents a breakout hit for you.

We regularly exceed this goal, but it's good to keep track and determine when content really is getting noticed. Ideally I'd love to see all 10 posts get more than 50 tweets.

Content Strategy Update

It's a good idea to review your content strategy every month and ensure it's all still making sense. Is it working in practice as well as it should in theory? Do you need to tweak some elements to further cement your differentiated position?

Key Relationships Update

Revisit your list of key relationships and look at any events that happened during the month. Did you get some good support from one of them? Has one of them gone quiet? Look at Google Analytics and see who is sending you traffic. Do you need to reach out and thank someone who has supported you? Do you need to update the list with new influencers? It pays to keep this list healthy and up-to-date.

Key Audience Comments

It's also good to take note of comments that prove your content is resonating. Document a few of the best comments from the month and note what makes them the most significant. Look out for evidence that people are really relating to your content or really using what you are putting out.

Content Promotion

We all dream about being able to create a piece of content and have it automatically explode and go viral. This won't happen to most people, and even relatively successful blogs still have to spend some time on content promotion.

Early on you might be a lot more actively involved, but you can taper it off as you grow.

There are literally hundreds, if not thousands, of things you can do to promote your content. What I find works is a simple procedure that an admin person or virtual assistant can follow and apply to all content. Then, for special content, you might have extra rules that you kick in for additional traction.

Here is a simple framework for promoting content. You can download the process at http://contentmachine.com/resources, and you can also check out a plethora of further resources related to content promotion. The process comes with a "procedures" document and a template for you or your team to utilize in every post. Here is a general description of what is included.

Lead Magnets

If you think it's going to be a popular piece of content, you might want to make a post-specific opt in. Remember: if you have set up the monthly check for your admin team, it will be picked up in Analytics anyway if it's a big hit. But it doesn't hurt to set this up from the start for important evergreen topics.

Check The Retargeting Funnel Category

Remember the retargeting funnel. If you've set it up properly, it will automatically retarget people with ads and emails if you post content in certain categories. If this is a major piece of content, and it's based around your core topics, then remember to add it to the necessary category to ensure people get retargeted.

Graphic Creation

Take a quote from the piece of content and find a related image. Use Canva or WordSwag to create two different images (you can get the image from the post or a background from these sites) with the quote for the blog post.

In our business we have the admin team do this task and get approval from the content manager on which image to use.

You can use these images on social media channels like Facebook or Instagram.

Create Click to Tweet

We choose a quotable phrase from the post to use as a "Click to Tweet". You can create one by logging into **Click to Tweet** (http://clicktotweet.com) with your Twitter account and following the steps to create the link. Make sure you include a link to your post in the actual tweet. That's a rookie mistake I've made more than once!

We then add the "Click to Tweet" into the actual post in the following format:

"Here is the body text for the tweet"
CLICK TO TWEET THIS

Mentions Tweets

If we have mentioned someone in the article, we want to draft some "mentions tweets". Log into your Twitter client of choice (I'd suggest Twitter itself, or Hootsuite or Buffer) and schedule tweets with three people per tweet like:

Mentions in [post name] on [main topic] [@guest1] [@ guest2] and [@guest3] [link]

I don't like to overdo these, so I wouldn't constantly do them for the same person or do them for more than a few people for each post.

Scheduled Tweets

We also schedule a bunch of tweets for each piece of content. We come up with a few different tweets based on the content and manually post them at intervals after the content is published. We use **Hootsuite** (https://hootsuite.com/) to schedule the tweets, but you can also use Buffer to auto-schedule them.

I don't like to be too aggressive with this, because I think it's annoying to see constant tweets about the same topic. I unfollow most twitter accounts tweeting like that. Normally we will only have three to four tweets for each piece of content, but in rare cases you might have more, so I've provided for more below.

- Quotable from click to tweet: When the post is published
- Tweet 1: Four hours after the post time
- Tweet 2: Post time + one day and one hour
- Tweet 3: Post time + seven days and two hours
- Tweet 4: Post time + 14 days and three hours
- Tweet 5: Post time + eight hours
- Tweet 6: Post time + two days and nine hours
- Tweet 7: Post time + 11 days and eight hours
- Tweet 8: Post time + three days and two hours
- Tweet 9: Post time + 12 hours
- Tweet 10: Post time + five days and 30 minutes
- Tweet 11+: Auto-schedule (for any more tweets we would just use the auto schedule feature)

Facebook Page

We also post our articles to Facebook. Sometimes I will post it to my personal account or to one of the groups which typically gets a lot more traction. We also paste the images and links to the main WP Curve Facebook page. While our actual page doesn't get a huge amount of traction, Facebook is still our number one social referrer, so we don't underestimate it.

Google Plus

We don't have a Google+ page, only my personal account. That means we can't currently auto post to it from Hootsuite or Buffer, so we do it manually.

- Visit Google+.
- Paste the link into the "Share what's new" box. It should automatically pick up the title and the image.
- Click Share.

Social Media Groups

If you are active in social media groups that allow sharing your own content, you can also post the articles to those groups. Forums are the same, although often forums will discourage members from blatantly posting their own content.

Content Submission Sites

There are also lots of sites that exist solely for people to submit and even "vote up" content. We keep a list of these sites, and when we do new posts, we log in and add our content. It is always better to be a good community member if it's a community site, so make sure to pay attention to other relevant pieces that are shared and upvote them as well.

Anything Post-Specific

The promotion steps above are intended as general steps to take with every piece of content. Often the best way to promote content will relate specifically to the content itself. We've had quite a few instances where we've done one small thing that has had a huge impact on the success of a post.

I wrote one post about Google Analytics reports, and we tweeted the official Google Analytics account to let them know. The next thing we knew, they tweeted it out, and the article quickly garnered more than 800 shares and thousands of views.

A similar thing happened when we wrote an article about monthly reports and included Buffer in the article. We tweeted them to let them know, and they added it to the "Content Suggestions" section in Buffer. The article ended up getting over 1,100 tweets—five times more than any article I've ever done on the site.

There are also other types of content that I often feel much more confident asking people to share. For example: we ran a content marketing survey, and because it's good for the industry, I had no problem asking a bunch of big online influencers to share the survey. We went from 18 completions to 51 completions in one day when influencers like Neil Patel, Hiten Shah, and Rob Walling shared the survey.

Paid Promotion

You can also use paid promotion to boost your content. A few simple options are:

1. Paid Facebook ads. Either use the ultra simple"'Boost Post" or a more complex ads manager.
2. Paid Twitter promotion.
3. Outbrain recommended articles network.

It's very difficult to determine the return on investment in paid content advertising. We don't do a lot of it, but it's an easy way to give something an extra boost.

Anything Else?

There are thousands of articles online dedicated to promoting content. I suggest starting with a simple process like the one I've presented here. Read up on some other options as well, and learn what works for you.

The important part is: don't forget to do it, and don't be too aggressive or spammy with your promotion methods. Keep in mind that you will probably have to do more of this early on, then less as you get more established.

Build The Team

Ultimately, to build a long-term content strategy that grows and prospers, you will have to build a content team. I've talked already about the importance of administrative staff or virtual assistants in a range of processes surrounding content marketing, but these are the two essential general roles of an effective content team: a Content Marketing Manager and Content Creators.

Content Marketing Manager

The Content Marketing Manager's job is to oversee your entire process of creating, publishing, and promoting content. In our company the Content Marketing Manager is supported by a team of admin staff and an external team of guest writers (Content Creators).

The Content Marketing Manager writes some of the content using the procedures in this book and also oversees the process of working with the guest writers.

The ideal person pays strong attention to detail, is friendly and personable with your audience, and can focus on creating long and high-quality content based on your guidelines.

As I mentioned before, I set some simple goals for our Content Marketing Manager:

1. 10 posts published per month.
2. One breakout hit of 50+ tweets per month.
3. A 5% growth in traffic each month.
4. A 5% growth in email opt in conversions.

Generally, our Content Marketing Manager will create six posts, and guest writers will create four. However, from time to time I want more attention given to things like lead magnets, so we will get more guest writers to help out that month.

Our Content Marketing Manager also sends the weekly email, which tells our audience about one piece of content for that week. We will usually pick the one we think has maximum chance of getting traction.

If your processes are structured well enough, then managing content marketing in this way is a trainable skill. As long as the person has a good attitude and the ability to focus and produce high-quality content, then you should be able to train up someone who's just getting started in the industry to do this role.

Content Creators

You also need people to create the content for you. Your Content Marketing Manager will do some of it, and you or your team may do some of it as well. I like to work with guest writers, because it's easy to scale up and down as we need more or less content.

The best way I've found to work with external content creators is by first choosing high-quality writers and then presenting very clear processes for working with you.

We've already been through using style guides for your content to work with external writers. Generally the way we manage guest writers is to have a pool of, say, six to eight regular writers and have a set of ideas that they can run with. Some writers will take those ideas, and some will come up with their own.

We use Trello to hold all of the ideas, and writers assign themselves to an idea if they want to take it.

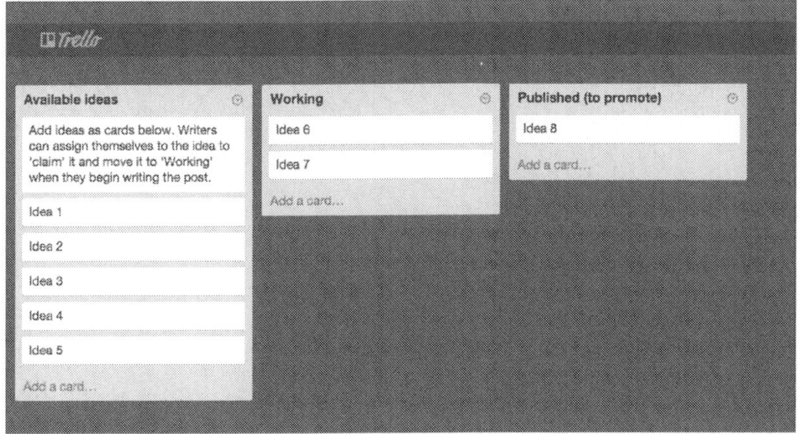

There are a lot of places you can find freelance writers to help out. Our best method was finding people through our own audience and people who have written guest posts for other blogs we like. Those people are often the best because they don't need fundamental training about what high-quality content is.

The main key here is to not accept content that doesn't match your standards. I've turned down content from some of my mentors that I thought wasn't high enough quality for our site. Sometimes we've rewritten posts and turned them into co-written pieces if we couldn't get what we wanted out of the guest writer. In the end, it's your audience and your responsibility to make sure the high standards are maintained.

Some guest writers will nail it straight away, and some won't make the cut. Keep an eye on who is getting traction and who isn't.

Almost There

Well done—you are almost there! In the last chapter, I'll quickly summarize the lessons to set you on your path of content marketing success.

EPILOGUE

WHERE TO GO FROM HERE?

Wherever you are in your content marketing journey, I hope you have taken away something valuable from this book.

You are so lucky that you are smack bang in the middle of a time when it's possible to build a seven-figure business without spending a cent on advertising. That's pretty awesome, and the fact that your competitors probably haven't clued in on this chance yet is even better.

Remember to value quality over quantity. Your content doesn't have to be Red-Bull-sideways-driving video level, but it has to be high quality. You get there by understanding the fundamentals, playing to your strengths, and being in tune with what your audience wants.

To build a real content machine you have to nail content quality, differentiation, and scale. Constantly monitor your progress and revisit your strategy if it's not working. Something *will* stick if you give it time and commit to the "content marketing leap of faith".

Make sure there is a logical step between your content and your business and don't forget your business fundamentals. Great content can't help grow a fundamentally bad business.

Remember that things don't scale without automation and delegation. Use the resources and frameworks in this book to make your life easier and build a content machine designed to scale. You can download free documents from http://contentmachine.com/resources on anything from generating ideas and developing them into content items, all the way through to writing style guidelines and content promotion lists.

Most of all, enjoy creating your content, telling your story, and building your community. You are doing a good thing by helping people and adding value to the world.

Be Part Of The 5% That Gets Shit Done

I've noticed one common trait in every successful entrepreneur I know. It's something I don't see in the rest of the population, and it's what makes them entrepreneurs. It's their relentless focus on delivering something. Getting shit done.

Ninety-five percent of people will happily read a book, maybe even take notes, but they don't measure themselves based on what they deliver. They won't change anything.

Five percent of people do. They are the entrepreneurs. It's not enough for them to read a book. It only matters when they deliver something as a result. Maybe it's implementing a new content strategy, testing out a new type of article, or brainstorming some new ideas for their blog.

If you DO something after reading this book, then I've succeeded. If you don't, then I've failed.

To make this happen, I've created a completely free Facebook group called The 7 Day Startup Group. It's filled with entrepreneurs and content creators who are actively building their content machines. We have thousands of members, and every day we discuss strategies from my first book and this one, and we help each other build our content machines and grow our businesses.

One of the biggest topics is how people are approaching social media. It changes so often that including it in the book would have made this content redundant in a few months. There are, instead, daily discussions in the group on best practices for social media.

Type '7 Day Startup' into Facebook, or visit http://contentmachine.com/resources and join us in building your content machine today. Tell us what one thing you actioned in the book and become part of the 5% of entrepreneurial content marketers who are getting shit done.

Do You Mind Helping?

I put a lot into this book, including quite a bit of my own money. If you got something out of it, I would absolutely love it if you could let the world know. There are two easy ways to do this.

First, if you could leave a review on Amazon, it really helps with rankings and sales. You can do that by first visiting http://contentmachine.com/amazon or searching for "Content Machine" on Amazon, and then writing a review. Even a quick note is fine and certainly appreciated.

Second, you can help by sharing http://contentmachine.com with friends or on social media with the hashtag #contentmachine. I like to share things that add value for my audience when they pop up, so I'll be watching this hashtag closely on Twitter and Instagram.

I'd also love for you to stay in touch with me. The best ways to do so are:

- Jump on my weekly email list at http://dannorris.me. I read and reply to all of my emails.

- Friend or follow me on Facebook at http://facebook.com/dannorrisinformly. I'll accept all friend requests until I reach the limit.
- Follow me on Twitter, Instagram or Periscope at @thedannorris.

ACKNOWLEDGEMENTS

Bret Thomson (http://www.bretthomson.com/) ran into me in the office and said "You should write a book about content marketing". Thanks for the idea Bret, here it is!

My co-founders are the reason I've been able to create the businesses I have. Thanks to Alex (**WP Curve** [http://wpcurve.com]), Luke (**Helloify** [http://helloify.com/]), and Eddie and Govs (**Black Hops Brewing** [http://blackhops.com.au/]).

Elisa Doucette and her team at **Craft Your Content** (http://www.craftyourcontent.com/) edited the book. Believe me—that's no easy task!

Derek Murphy designed the cover, and he also bought me a shirt that says "Published Author". Haha, what a legend. Check out Derek's work at **CreativIndie Covers** (http://creativindiecovers.com).

Chris O'Byrne from **JETLAUNCH** (http://jetlaunch.net) formatted the entire book for me and made it sexy for Amazon.

Tom Morkes (http://tommorkes.com) is a book-marketing and self-publishing legend and all-around hustler and good bloke. He led the marketing for this book and my first book and if you are reading this, he did a good job!

Kyle Gray, my Content Marketing Manager at WP Curve, has contributed a lot of content to this book and helped me review and improve it. He's also been active in the 7 Day Startup Facebook group and has implemented a lot of these ideas for WP Curve, as I've written the book. Thanks Kyle, I really appreciate it, mate.

Thanks to all of the entrepreneurs and groups who have inspired me over the years including: Brendon Sinclair, Adam Franklin, Toby Jenkins, James Schramko, Chris Ducker, Neil Patel, Hiten Shah, Joe Pulizzi, John Lee Dumas, Lewis Howes, James Altucher, Jason Calacanis, Noah Kagan, Dan Andrews, Mark Manson, Elisa Doucette, Kathryn Minshew, Alex Turnbull, Taylor Pearson, Tim Reid, Ross Beard, Greg Ciotti, Clay Collins, Chris Hexton, Wade Foster, Marcus Sheridan, Joel Gascoigne, Kevan Lee, Peep Laja, Justin Cooke and Joe Magnotti, Jason Cohen, Rand Fishkin, Rob Walling, Josh Pigford, Tim Conley, Jake Hower, Kevin Rogers, Seth Godin, Alex Blumburg, Darren Rouse, Troy Dean, Rob Walling, Tim Ferriss, Pat Flynn, Mike

Taber, Belle Beth Cooper, Natalie Sisson, Erica Douglass, Sean Ellis, James Farmer and the team at WPMU, Aaron Agius, Nikki Durkin, Brian Casel, Ed Dale, Laura Roeder, Joanna and the team at CopyHackers, Matt, Joelle and the team at How to Build a Rocketship, Andrew Warner, Trent Dyrsmid, Damian Thompson, Gideon Shalwick, David Nihil, Kevin Rogers, Matt Ruby, Gary Vaynerchuk, Marie Forleo, Ana Hoffman, Allan Branch, Robert Gerrish and the team at Flying Solo, Corbett Barr and the team at Fizzle, Brian and the team at CopyBlogger, Des and the team at Intercom, Greg and the team at Help Scout, Georgina and the team at Unbounce, Renee and Heather at Onboardly and Mat and Tas at Startup Daily.

A special thanks to the members of the Facebook group who have been an awesome support to me while putting this book together.

Finally, thank you for reading the book and undertaking a type of marketing that adds value to the world.

Happy creating. :)

BIBLIOGRAPHY

"2013 Search Engine Ranking Factors." Moz. SEOmoz, Inc. http://moz.com/search-ranking-factors.

Amazon. Amazon.com, Inc. http://Amazon.com.

Andrews, Dan and Ian Schoen. *Tropical MBA* (blog). Tropical MBA. http://tropicalmba.com.

Asprey, Dave. Bulletproof. Bulletproof Digital, Inc. https://www.bulletproofexec.com/.

Beeche, Mat. "After only 18 months in business Frank Body will likely exceed $20 million in revenue this year." *Startup Daily*. Last modified February 25, 2015. http://www.startupdaily.net/2015/02/18-months-business-frank-body-will-likely-exceed-20-million-revenue-year/.

Bell, Aaron. AdRoll. AdRoll.com. http://Adroll.com.

Beykpour, Kayvon and Joe Bernstein. Periscope. Twitter, Inc. https://www.periscope.tv/about.

Blackwell, James and Henley Wing. BuzzSumo. http://buzzsumo.com.

Buffer. https://buffer.com/.

Calacanis, Jason. Inside. http://inside.com.

________. Launch Festival. http://www.launchfestival.com/.

________. *This Week in Startups* (podcast). Launch Media, LLC. http://thisweekinstartups.com/.

Canva. http://canva.com.

Carnahan. Shawn and Dan Castles. ScreenFlow. Telestream, LLC. http://telestream.net/screenflow/overview.htm.

Chestnut, Ben and Dan Kurzius. MailChimp. The Rocket Science Group. http://mailchimp.com.

Chicola, Jason. Rev. Rev.com. https://www.rev.com/.

Ching, Ai and Andrea. Piktochart. Piktochart Infographics. http://piktochart.com/.

ClickToTweet. http://clicktotweet.com.

Conrad, Neal, and Drew. *The Wine Wankers* (blog). http://thewinewankers.com.au/.

Cooper, Belle Beth. "How Twitter's Expanded Images Increase Clicks, Retweets and Favorites [New Data]." *Buffer Social* (blog). Buffer. Last modified November 13, 2013. https://blog.bufferapp.com/the-power-of-twitters-new-expanded-images-and-how-to-make-the-most-of-it.

Coursera. Coursera, Inc. https://www.coursera.org/.

Daniels, Matthew. "The Largest Vocabulary in Hip Hop." Last modified June 2014. http://rappers.mdaniels.com.s3-website-us-east-1.amazonaws.com/.

"DC SHOES: KEN BLOCK'S GYMKHANA FIVE: ULTIMATE URBAN PLAYGROUND; SAN FRANCISCO." YouTube video. Posted by DC Shoes. July 9, 2012. https://www.youtube.com/watch?v=LuDN2bCIyus.

Disqus. https://disqus.com/.

Doucette, Elisa. Craft Your Content. http://www.craftyourcontent.com/.

________. *Shattering Glass. Forbes* online. http://www.forbes.com/sites/elisadoucette/.

________. "The Art Of Online Apologies And Why Elizabeth Lauten Failed Miserably At Hers." *Shattering Glass. Forbes* online. Last modified December 1, 2014. http://www.forbes.com/sites/elisadoucette/2014/11/30/the-art-of-apologies-and-why-elizabeth-lauten-failed-miserably-at-hers/.

Dry, Justin and Andre Eikmeier. Vinomofo. WineCru. http://vinomofo.com/content/articles.

Dumas, John Lee. Entrepreneur on Fire. http://www.entrepreneuronfire.com/.

Ecamm Call Recorder. Ecamm Network, LLC. http://www.ecamm.com/mac/callrecorder/.

Ferriss, Timothy. The 4-Hour Workweek. http://fourhourworkweek.com/.

Flynn, Pat. "SPI 071: Successful Start Ups, Millions Lost and Everything In-Between: Inside the Mind of Noah Kagan from AppSumo." *The Smart Passive Income Blog* (blog). Flynndustries, LLC. June 19, 2013. http://

www.smartpassiveincome.com/spi-071-successful-start-ups-millions-lost-and-everything-in-between-inside-the-mind-of-noah-kagan-from-appsumo/.

———. *The Smart Passive Income Blog* (blog). Flynndustries, LLC. http://www.smartpassiveincome.com/.

Followerwonk. SEOmoz, Inc. https://followerwonk.com/.

For The Love And Money. Love + Money Pty Ltd. http://fortheloveandmoney.com.

Forleo, Marie. Marie Forleo International. http://marieforleo.com.

Frank Body. http://frankbody.com.

———. Instagram. http://instagram.com/frank_bod.

French, Katy. Visage (blog). http://visage.co/. "Kurt Vonnegut Graphs the Shapes of Stories." Last Modified August 13, 2014. http://visage.co/kurt-vonnegut-shows-us-shapes-stories/

FunnyBizz (blog). http://funnybizz.co/.

Geraerts, Erika and Jess Hatzis. Willow and Blake. http://willowandblake.com.

GifGrabber. http://www.gifgrabber.com/.

Godin, Seth. http://www.sethgodin.com/.

Google Adwords: Keyword Planner. Google. https://adwords.google.com/KeywordPlanner.

Google Analytics. Google. http://google.com/analytics.

Google Forms. Google. http://www.google.com/forms/.

Google Trends. Google. http://google.com/trends.

Google Webmasters. Google.
https://www.google.com/webmasters/.

Google+ Hangouts. Google.
http://www.google.com/hangouts.

Goraly, Gilad and Rami Goraly. ScheduleOnce.
http://scheduleonce.com.

Hamilton, William. Camtasia. TechSmith Corporation.
http://techsmith.com/camtasia.html.

———. Jing. TechSmith Corporation.
http://techsmith.com/jing.html.

Harbottle, Mark and Matt Mickiewicz. 99designs.
http://99Designs.com.

Harris, Bryan. Video Fruit. http://videofruit.com.

Helmig, Bryan Wade Foster, and Mike Knoop. Zapier.
Zapier Inc. https://zapier.com.

HelpScout (blog). http://www.helpscout.net/blog/.

Holmes, Ryan. HootSuite. https://hootsuite.com/.

Inkybee. Forth Metrics Ltd. http://www.inkybee.com/.

Inside Intercom (blog). Intercom. https://blog.intercom.io/.

Instagram. https://instagram.com/.

Kagan, Noah. AppSumo. http://appsumo.com.

———. OK Dork. http://okdork.com.

———. SumoMe, AppSumo, http://sumome.com.

Klout. Klout, Inc. https://klout.com.

LeadPages. http://leadpages.com.

Like Explorer. http://likeexplorer.com.

Little Bird. Little Bird Technologies.
http://www.getlittlebird.com/.

Long, Adam and Ben Long. Hemmingway Editor. http://www.hemingwayapp.com/.

Lucidchart. Lucid Software Inc. http://lucidchart.com.

Lunden, Ingrid. "Tumblr Overtakes Instagram As Fastest-Growing Social Platform, Snapchat Is

The Fastest-Growing App." *TechCrunch*. AOL Inc. Last modified November 25. 2014. http://techcrunch.com/2014/11/25/tumblr-overtakes-instagram-as-fastest-growing-social-platform-snapchat-is-the-fastest-growing-app/.

Mask, Clate and Scott Martineau. Infusionsoft. http://infusionsoft.com.

McClafferty, Alex and Dan Norris. WP Curve. http://wpcurve.com/.

Medium. A Medium Corporation. http://medium.com.

Meetup. http://meetup.com.

Meme Generator. http://memegenerator.net.

Mention. http://mention.net.

Morkes, Tom. http://tommorkes.com.

Murphy, Derek. CreativIndie Covers. Creativindie Book Covers. http://www.creativindiecovers.com/.

Norris, Dan. Amazon. Amazon.com, Inc., http://www.amazon.com/Dan-Norris/e/B00O0H6T2M.

________. Content Machine. http://contentmachine.com/.

________. http://contentmachine.com/resources/.

________. Facebook. http://facebook.com/dannorrisinformly.

________. http://dannorris.me/.

________. Instagram. https://instagram.com/thedannorris/.

________. Twitter. Twitter, Inc. https://twitter.com/thedannorris.

O'Byrne, Chris. JetLaunch: Strategic Self Publishing. http://www.jetlaunch.net/.

OKCupid. Humor Rainbow, Inc. http://www.okcupid.com/.

Oldfield, Eddie, Michael McGovern, and Dan Norris. Black Hops Brewing. http://blackhops.com.au/.

OptinSkin. http://optinskin.com.

Pamela for Skype. PamConsult. http://www.pamela.biz/.

Patel, Neil. *Kissmetrics* (blog). http://blog.kissmetrics.com/.

________. *The Daily Egg* (blog). http://blog.crazyegg.com/.

________. Quick Sprout. Quick Sprout, LLC. http://www.quicksprout.com/.

Peretti, Jonah. BuzzFeed. BuzzFeed, Inc. http://buzzfeed.com.

Pulizzi, Joe. "New B2B Content Marketing Research: Focus on Documenting Your Strategy." *Content Marketing Institute*. Z Squared Media LLC. Last modified October 1, 2014. http://contentmarketinginstitute.com/2014/10/2015-b2b-content-marketing-research/.

Quora. http://quora.com.

Reddit. Reddit Inc. http://reddit.com.

Relately. http://relate.ly/.

Rogers, Kevin. *The 60-Second Sales Hook*. http://60second saleshook.com.

Rogers, Simon. "What fuels a Tweet's engagement?" *Twitter Blog* (blog). Twitter, Inc. Last modified March 10, 2014. https://blog.twitter.com/2014/what-fuels-a-tweets-engagement.

Ronalds, Luke and Dan Norris. Helloify. http://helloify.com/.

Ruby, Matt. Vooza. http://vooza.com/.

Skitch. Evernote Corporation. https://evernote.com/skitch/.

SlideShare. LinkedIn Corporation. http://www.slideshare.net/.

Snapchat. Snapchat, Inc. https://www.snapchat.com/.

The Moz Blog (blog). SEOmoz.com, Inc. https://moz.com/blog.

The Muse. Daily Muse, Inc. http://themuse.com.

Theme Forest. Envato Pty Ltd. http://themeforest.net.

Thomson, Bret. http://www.bretthomson.com/.

Trello. Trello, Inc. http://trello.com/.

Turnbull, Alex. *Groove* (blog). https://www.groovehq.com/blog.

Twitter. Twitter, Inc. http://twitter.com.

Udemy. Udemy.com. https://www.udemy.com/.

Vaynerchuk, Gary. SlideShare. LinkedIn Corporation. http://www.slideshare.net/vaynerchuk/.

Vine. Vine Labs, Inc. https://vine.co/.

Visme. Easy WebContent, Inc. http://visme.co/.

Wong, Ben. WordSwag. Oringe. http://wordswag.co.

Woodman, Angus. Crew. https://crew.co/.

Yoast. Joost de Valk - Yoast.com. Yoast BV. https://yoast.com/wordpress/plugins/seo/.

YouTube Live. YouTube, LLC. https://www.youtube.com/.